*The Hollywood
Action and
Adventure Film*

NEW APPROACHES TO FILM GENRE

Series Editor: Barry Keith Grant

New Approaches to Film Genre provides students and teachers with original, insightful, and entertaining overviews of major film genres. Each book in the series gives an historical appreciation of its topic, from its origins to the present day, and identifies and discusses the important films, directors, trends, and cycles. Authors articulate their own critical perspective, placing the genre's development in relevant social, historical, and cultural contexts. For students, scholars, and film buffs alike, these represent the most concise and illuminating texts on the study of film genre.

THE HOLLYWOOD ACTION AND ADVENTURE FILM

Yvonne Tasker

WILEY Blackwell

This edition first published 2015
© 2015 John Wiley & Sons, Inc.

Registered Office
John Wiley & Sons, Ltd, The Atrium, Southern Gate, Chichester, West Sussex,
PO19 8SQ, UK

Editorial Offices
350 Main Street, Malden, MA 02148-5020, USA
9600 Garsington Road, Oxford, OX4 2DQ, UK
The Atrium, Southern Gate, Chichester, West Sussex, PO19 8SQ, UK

For details of our global editorial offices, for customer services, and for information about how
to apply for permission to reuse the copyright material in this book please see our website at
www.wiley.com/wiley-blackwell.

The right of Yvonne Tasker to be identified as the author of this work has been asserted in
accordance with the UK Copyright, Designs and Patents Act 1988.

Library of Congress Cataloging-in-Publication Data

Tasker, Yvonne, 1964–
    The Hollywood action and adventure film / Yvonne Tasker. – 1
      pages   cm. – (New approaches to film genre)
    Summary: "Provides a timely and richly revealing portrait of a powerful cinematic genre that
has increasingly come to dominate the American cinematic landscape" – Provided by publisher.
    Includes bibliographical references and index.
    ISBN 978-0-470-65924-3 (hardback) – ISBN 978-0-470-65925-0 (paper)   1. Action and
adventure films–United States–History and criticism.   I. Title.
    PN1995.9.A3T37 2015
    791.43′6582–dc23
                                                    2014047943

A catalogue record for this book is available from the British Library.

Sylvester Stallone in Rambo 3, 1988 (dir. Peter McDonald). CAROLCO / THE KOBAL
COLLECTION

Set in 11/13.5pt Bembo by SPi Publisher Services, Pondicherry, India

Printed in Singapore by C.O.S. Printers Pte Ltd

1   2015

CONTENTS

LIST OF PLATES

ACKNOWLEDGMENTS

This short book has been researched and written over a number of years. During that time I've benefited enormously from discussions with friends and colleagues as fascinated by action and adventure cinema as I have been. While, as ever, errors are my own, I'd like to thank in particular Lisa Coulthard, Christine Holmlund, Eric Lichtenfeld, Lisa Purse and Lindsay Steenberg. Jenny Romero at the Margaret Herrick Library provided invaluable support at the research stage, while Barry Grant has been a patient and insightful editor. Thanks also to Jayne Fargnoli and Julia Kirk at Wiley-Blackwell. Finally heartfelt thanks to my partner Rachel Hall and to our twins, Amy and Henry; the three of you have shared fully in the action experience these last few years and the book is the better for it.

CHAPTER 1

ACTION AND ADVENTURE AS GENRE

This book explores action and adventure as a mode of filmmaking and as a significant genre of American cinema. What we call "action" today has generic roots in a number of surprisingly diverse aspects of Hollywood cinema, from early chase films that crafted suspense to travel films that offered to audiences exotic and fantastic spectacles of other lands. Making sense of action involves taking account of these diverse origins; conversely, thinking about action as a genre allows us to see those origins in a different way.

Action is now a generic descriptor in its own right, one closely linked to adventure cinema; it is widely used to promote and distribute films in theatres and for home use. Yet, however familiar it may now be, this designation is relatively recent. Those earlier Hollywood genres that strongly emphasize action elements – including war movies, Westerns and thrillers – have their own distinct generic histories and conventions. It is not my intention here to suggest we think about all these movies as action, but rather to draw attention to action

The Hollywood Action and Adventure Film, First Edition. Yvonne Tasker.
© 2015 John Wiley & Sons, Inc. Published 2015 by John Wiley & Sons, Inc.

and adventure as long established features of Hollywood production as well as that of other national cinemas. In the process we will understand the longevity of action movies and how action emerges as a distinct genre during the "New Hollywood" of the 1970s, with its orientation around high concept, pre-sold blockbusters.

Associated with narratives of quest and discovery, and spectacular scenes of combat, violence and pursuit, action and adventure films have been produced throughout Hollywood's history. They are not restricted to any particular historical or geographic setting (which provided the basis for early iconographic models of genre). Indeed, the basic elements of physical conflict, chase and challenge can be inflected in any number of different directions. Action can be comic, graphically violent, fantastic, apocalyptic, military, conspiratorial and even romantic.

Action and adventure cinemas thus pose something of a challenge to genre theory as it has developed within film studies. Despite the recognizability of particular action or adventure cycles – Warner Bros. historical adventures of the 1930s, say, or the bi-racial cop movies of the 1980s – the genre has no clear and consistent iconography or setting. There *are* some broadly consistent and identifiable themes underpinning action: these include the quest for freedom from oppression, say, or the hero's ability to use his/her body in overcoming enemies and obstacles. And physical conflicts or challenge, whether battling human or alien opponents or even hostile natural environments, are fundamental to the genre in all its manifestations. Yet the very diversity of action and adventure requires thinking about genre in a different way than the familiar analyses of more clearly defined genres such as the Western, which has been fruitfully explored in terms of its rendition of themes to do with the symbolic opposition of wilderness and civilization, nature and culture (Kitzes, 1969).

Adopting a genre-based approach to action doesn't mean reducing this diversity to a set formula: as if *Star Wars* (1977) were the same as *Die Hard* (1988), or *Strange Days* (1995) the same as *Speed* (1994). Action and adventure as cinematic forms are manifest in a multiplicity of different genres and sub-genres that develop and change over time. As such, action and adventure provides a useful way into ongoing debates regarding the *instability* of genre and the extent to which individual films can be regarded as participating simultaneously in a number of genres. So, to take these examples, we might agree that

Die Hard is quite different from *Star Wars*, but note that both *Star Wars* and *Strange Days* make use of science-fiction conventions. Yet these two films do so in very different ways – notably in the presentation of violence – and in combination with other generic elements.

Star Wars exemplifies a resurgent adventure strand of the 1970s cinema, its Jedi knights and light sabers, as well as set-piece scenes such as characters swinging on ropes between platforms, recalling the swordfights of swashbuckling films. *Star Wars* also deploys western iconography via (admittedly alien) desert landscapes and in particular through Han Solo (Harrison Ford)'s costume and mannerisms. All this takes place in juxtaposition with the sort of science fiction evoked by the imagery of space travel as routine and spectacular space battles. *Star Wars* places its futuristic scenario in relation to genres defined by their pastness: "a long time ago…" *Strange Days*, by contrast, is set in the near future (now the past) of 1999. It employs intense mobile camerawork to evoke chase and pursuit in its action sequences. The futuristic technology portrayed is to do with vision and the recording of experiences; the film uses salacious imagery alongside its conspiratorial thriller and *film noir* elements. While both movies can be situated as part of action and adventure traditions, understanding the diversity of filmmaking styles is important to analyzing the genre.

Given action's diverse history and its complex relationship to other genres, such as the Western or science-fiction, this book considers action both as an overarching term and in relation to a series of sub-genres. This chapter gives an overview of some of the main ways in which genre has been theorized in film studies and asks about how these different approaches might help in thinking about action and adventure. Since "action" *per se* has not been central to genre theory, this involves acknowledging the specific context used by critics (e.g., Bazin on the Western) while summarizing the relevance of these debates for an understanding of action as genre.

Theories of Genre: Author, Icon and Industry

The development of genre criticism represented a crucial stage in the emergence of film studies as a discipline and was particularly important in its attempt to engage with popular and especially Hollywood cinema during the 1950s and 1960s. Given the typically low critical status accorded to action and adventure movies (a few notable exceptions aside) this is also a particularly important context for the subsequent emergence of scholarship around the genre. Seminal essays published in the 1940s and 1950s by French critic André Bazin and American writer Robert Warshow developed interest in genre via evocative accounts of the cultural work and relevance of the Western and the gangster film, both action-oriented genres.

These early essays are intriguing since they foreground the cultural significance of these genres, largely in terms of the assumed connections between genre filmmaking and myth. Thus, Bazin regards the Western as exemplifying American film in articulating values to do with "establishing justice and respect for the law" (1995: 145). For Warshow, the gangster film is significant not for any relation to social reality but as an *aesthetic experience* that speaks against what he regards as the compulsory optimism of American life: "the gangster speaks for us, expressing that part of the American psyche which rejects the qualities and the demands of modern life, which rejects 'Americanism' itself" (1964: 86). Approaching Hollywood films for what they can tell us about social values and systems of meaning – that is, myth and ideology – has proved central to writings on action. Indeed until relatively recently, an interest in the ideology of action has tended to be at the cost of more sustained discussion of the formal elements that make the genre so distinctive and, arguably, popular.

For Bazin the distinctive achievement of the Western lies not in action elements, though he acknowledges their importance, but in its articulation of myth. Thus he writes:

> It is easy to say that because the cinema is movement the western is cinema *par excellence*. It is true that galloping horses and fights are its usual ingredients. But in that case the western would simply be one variety of adventure story. (1995: 141)

Here, Bazin asserts unequivocally that the Western's significance lies not in its dynamic visual elements or in its adventure-driven narratives. Chapter 3 addresses in more detail the different ways in which critics have explored both the ideological work and, latterly, aesthetic aspects of action and adventure cinema. Here, we can note a persistent feature of criticism surrounding action genres; an ambivalence about cultural value. While across decades critics have understood the exhilarating properties of action, disagreements proceed from what significance (and what value) should be accorded to such cinematic sensuality. For Brian Taves, for example, adventure cinema is "something beyond action," elevated "beyond the physical challenge" by "its moral and intellectual flavour." (1993: 12). By implication action is crude, a framework that requires gifted filmmakers and performers to transcend its conventions. Indeed for those writers, such as Wheeler Winston Dixon, who regret "the paucity of imagination and/or risk in Hollywood cinema," (1998: 182) action is among the forms of mega-budget, effects-heavy filmmaking that has come to symbolize what they regard as a loss of meaning and complexity.

By contrast, Warshow writes that "the gangster film is simply one example of the movies' constant tendency to create fixed dramatic patterns that can be repeated indefinitely with a reasonable expectation of profit," while being clear that this "rigidity is not necessarily opposed to the requirements of art." (1964: 85). Indeed thinking about genre, with its emphasis on formulae and repetition, has encouraged film scholars to give more attention to the commercial and institutional aspects of film production. Whether the focus is industry or aesthetics, critics tend to agree that genre is distinguished by patterns of repetition and difference. Thus genre critics are interested in the visual, narrative and thematic patterns that recur over time as well as taking account of the ways in which film texts vary those patterns.

Iconographic models of genre emphasized the continuity provided by recurrent scenes and signs. Colin McArthur's well-known work on the gangster film foregrounds (1972) processes whereby repetition generates familiarity, but just as importantly allows objects and actions to accrue meaning through that very repetition. So, for instance, genre critics have noted the resonance and meaning of signs such as landscape, horses and guns in the Western. For action the key sign is the movement of the body through space; the body is central to action whether it is superhuman or simply enhanced. Heroic bodies both withstand and inflict violence. They are juxtaposed with an iconography of violence stemming from the weapon as accessory. Both the action body and action spectacle is characterized by movement: from the lengthy depictions of pursuit and combat to the explosions that feature so prominently in action spectacle. Explosions are a generic expectation of action turning on the movement of billowing flames and of the objects thrown up or buildings imploded by the blast. The familiar action image of the hero's body propelled by a blast effectively couples both forms of movement, his/her survival underlining their strength and suitability for violence.

Of course as noted earlier, action and adventure are broad descriptors when set against even a genre as expansive as the Western. Eric Lichtenfeld rightly draws attention to the fascination with weaponry that characterizes gunplay-heavy contemporary Hollywood action, for instance, suggesting that an "enthusiasm for action film modernity" in John Wayne's *McQ* (1974) is typified by a "zeal for weaponry." (2004: 31) Modern Hollywood action and adventure is as likely to suggest a fascination at work with the body as a weapon – in part a consequence of the influence of Asian martial arts and the genres showcasing them – and the exploitation of fantastical/historical settings that require different forms of weaponry. The swordplay of *Pirates of the Caribbean* (2003) is different from, say, the stunts and digital effects conveying superhuman prowess in the same year's *X2*.

PLATE 1.1 Action cinema's characteristic "zeal for weaponry" (Lichtenfeld) and the weaponized body: Fox (Angelina Jolie) in *Wanted* (2008, directed by Timur Bekmambetov and produced by Universal Pictures, Spyglass Entertainment, Relativity Media, Marc Platt Productions, Kickstart Productions, Top Cow Productions, Ringerike Zweite Filmproduktion and Bazelevs Production).

Under the influence of structuralism in the 1970s, scholars explored genre primarily as a system built on repetition and variation (although the work of individual filmmakers – which auteurism construed in comparable terms of repetition and innovation – was still privileged). Anthropology was an important disciplinary context for this work, as film and the developing field of cultural studies looked to the work of Claude Levi-Strauss among others, arguing for a view of popular film (and popular culture more widely) as examples of myth and ritual. So Schatz theorized genre as myth, foregrounding "the various stories our culture tells itself to purify and justify the values and beliefs which sustain it" (1981: 263).

Action has been most often understood in this way, with critics foregrounding its significance as an ideological sign of the times. Indeed it was only with the establishment of a more anthropological interest in popular cinema – by which critics began to investigate popular culture as key markers of social and ideological values – that action and adventure, genres seemingly without clear claims to value on aesthetic grounds, could effectively enter critical debates. As I'll discuss in Chapter 3, many critics have seen the commercial prominence of action, and its emergence as a generic marker, since the 1980s as revealing of the ideological conservatism of Hollywood cinema. Action is read in terms of changes in the industry that saw increasing budgets in line with an emphasis on the blockbuster along with shifts towards new platforms and greater dependence on international box office.

The flurry of genre criticism that appeared from the 1960s frequently served as a sort of supplement to perspectives on film authorship; thus we see influential essays on John Ford or Howard Hawks' use of the Western, Ophuls' melodramas or Minelli's musicals. Thomas Schatz adopted Bazin's phrase the "genius of the system" to convey the aesthetic possibilities that genre cinema might offer to the filmmaker as auteur. In this view, genres were seen to provide filmmakers with a rich repertoire of images with which to work, allowing them to modify generic tropes and inflect familiar scenarios with subtle resonances.

Since neither action nor adventure has historically been seen as a strongly authored cinema, these cinematic traditions were effectively absent from such debates. Or, more accurately, critical discussion centered on genres such as the Western with little reference to their status as action or adventure stories. More recently this has shifted with interest in action-oriented filmmakers including Kathryn Bigelow and Quentin Tarantino, whose status as *auteurs* of action and violence features in popular commentary. Other filmmakers such as Steven Spielberg, James Cameron, Peter Jackson, Joel Silver and Michael Bay are just as often discussed as symptomatic of the operations of the film industry as in relation to the (in any case rather dated) framework of authorial vision.

The scale, expense and technological complexity – as well as the commercial successes – of the most high profile instances of action and adventure cinema underline the industrial, collaborative aspects of Hollywood production. To some extent then, interest in these filmmakers lies in – or at least must take account of – their command of the business of filmmaking as much as older models of authorial criticism that emphasized the repetition of visual and thematic markers. Writing in the 1970s on adventure cinema, Jeffrey Richards noted that,

> Since the way a swashbuckler moves and looks is just as important as what it says, we must look to the art director, costume designer, fencing master, stunt arranger, cinematographer and actor just as much as to writer and director. For the swashbuckler is truly the sum of all their work. (1977: 10)

While there is less interest in director-centered auteurism in contemporary film scholarship, the direction that Richards indicates has not been particularly developed. Nonetheless, in addition to being commercially lucrative, when action and adventure movies secure awards it is most often in categories such as visual effects and sound editing, a tendency that underlines the pertinence of Richards' remarks on the creative labor at work in the genre.

Theorizing Genre History: Evolution and Industry

If genre has to do with repetition and difference, genre cinema also develops, changing over time as, through repetition, some conventions become clichés. In turn, in many ways genre criticism is fundamentally a retrospective enterprise. Some genre histories are industrial in focus, others formal or cultural. In any case genre histories attempt to make sense of the ways in which movie conventions develop over time, become familiar through repetition, are inflected in new ways and – in some cases – seem to fall away. Evolutionary models of genre, such as that suggested by Thomas Schatz in his influential 1981 study *Hollywood Genres*, propose a movement by which genres are established, mature into a classic form and then shift to a mode defined by parody and self-reflexivity.

Schatz explores this cycle or pattern with reference to the Western, suggesting a redefinition of the genre shaped by the evolving historical context of the post-war period, often understood as a period defined by questioning as much as conformity.[1] The case studies presented here suggest a rather different model. Indeed action and adventure seem particularly resistant to this sort of evolutionary chronology; as I explore in Chapter 7, through a discussion of *Raiders of the Lost Ark* (1981) and *Pirates of the Caribbean* (2003), self-reflexivity has for decades been an important element in a genre that routinely recycles its own history, drawing on the conventions of other genres from horror to imperial adventure. Indeed as Brian Taves observes: "Because swashbucklers and pirate adventures often included humorous elements, the genre retains viability even as it is parodied" (1993: 81), a position he contrasts to that of the Western.

Historical perspectives on the "evolution" of genre are particularly interesting for thinking about action and adventure due to the longevity as well as the diversity of these forms. Ben Singer (2001) identifies action as a key element of silent cinema's chase films; as he notes, at the time these scenarios were termed melodrama. Steve Neale frames action-adventure as one of Hollywood cinema's major genres, underlining its long history as a counter to scholarly debates that have typically focused on a number of high profile titles released during and since the 1980s. Neale identifies the long standing use of action and adventure as promotional terms, indicating that "films in the action-adventure tradition have been a staple in Hollywood's output since the 1910s" (1999: 55).

---

[1]   In his essay "The Evolution of the Western," Bazin too identified World War II as a significant factor in the development of the Western.

Insisting on the longevity of these cinematic forms, Neale's analysis helps to reposition debates about action, which assumed the genre to be a phenomenon that represented the New Hollywood rather than the old. In the process Neale also points out the generic diversity that characterizes action:

> With its immediate roots in nineteenth-century melodrama and in a principle strand of popular fiction, action–adventure has always encompassed an array of genres and sub-types: Westerns, swashbucklers, war films, disaster films, space operas, epics, safari films, jungle films, and so on. (1999: 55)

This very diversity has doubtless contributed to action–adventure's relative invisibility in genre studies – it lacks the clarity of definition that is so productive for writings on the gangster film.

Elaborating the distinction between semantic (focusing on, say, iconographic generic markers) and syntactic (concerned with deep structures of meaning) approaches to genre, Rick Altman points out how the genres most commonly discussed by scholars are those that lend themselves to both approaches; he singles out the Western, horror and the musical as genres that possess both "a high degree of semantic recognisability and a high level of syntactic consistency" (2000: 90–91). Neither action nor adventure can be said to conform to this sort of recognizability and consistency. Thus, while Bazin may have observed in the 1950s, not inaccurately perhaps, that "[t]here is no difference between Hopalong Cassidy and Tarzan except for their costume and the arena in which they demonstrate their prowess" (1995, 143), there are, nonetheless, specificities to the Western and jungle adventure respectively. Which is also to say that costume and setting are more than superficial elements; setting them aside does little to facilitate the analysis of such films.

Evolutionary models of genre are often underpinned by a sense of how the film industry works. Crudely, an understanding that Hollywood invests in those genres that attract audiences is as important as the notion that what sells (what is popular) can tell us useful things about social values at any particular point. Schatz suggests both that genres serve as forms of "cultural ritual" and the public's "collective expression" of values, but also that they exemplify mass (rather than folk) culture (1981: 12). Industrial analyses of genre and film cycles are also instructive, as are an understanding of the limits posed by censorship and by technology (themes to which I return throughout this book). For example, Tino Balio's overview of the historical adventure cycle produced at Warner Bros. in the 1930s locates the development of these titles as, in part, the result of a series of circumstances. For some unknown reason star Robert Donat dropped out of Warners' production *Captain Blood* (1935), an adaptation of Sabatini's popular novel, and that the studio took a chance on the unknown Errol Flynn. On the back of the film's considerable commercial success, Flynn and Olivia de Havilland became stars. In turn, and in line with the developing logic of the industry, "Warners embarked on a cycle of costume-adventure pictures that combined the talents of Flynn with Olivia de Havilland and [director] Michael Curtiz" (1993: 203). The cycle includes *The Adventures of Robin Hood* that Balio, in line with the general view, regards as Flynn's finest film, in which the star "and his role were perfectly matched" (204).

In the New Hollywood that follows the dismantling of the studio system, different factors come into play in deciding which films are made and how they are developed. Yet commercial logic and box office success remain key with unexpected successes and shifts in star persona contributing to the process. Thus Bruce Willis' success as action hero John McClane in *Die Hard* (1988) was a significant change from his earlier television persona. Likewise, Johnny Depp's quirky characterization of pirate hero Captain Jack Sparrow in the *Pirates of the Caribbean* films played a significant part in the series' success, the distinctive costume and style facilitating associated delivering merchandising. Eric Lichtenfeld's authoritative study of the action movie takes account of the work of a range of personnel from publicists to editors and producers, acknowledging that many action films form the anchor for commercial franchises in which the film itself is only one element. Since budgets for action movies have grown significantly – the production budget for *The Hunger Games* (2012) was moderate at around $78 million, as against the same year's superhero hit *The Avengers* at $220 million – and as a consequence commercial pressures on production teams are intense.

Altman argues that "Hollywood regularly eschews genre logic for production and publicity decisions in favour of series, cycles, remakes and sequels" (2000: 115). These processes are certainly apparent in the history of action and adventure filmmaking, as several of the case study chapters make clear. *The Hunger Games* is an adaptation of the first book in a best-selling trilogy of novels by Suzanne Collins, the teenage readership a core target for the film. *The Avengers* brings together a number of Marvel comic characters featured in print and in prior movies. Both films are then effectively pre-sold. Nonetheless the series, cycles, remakes and sequels explored in this book also make sense within a larger generic context. Indeed I argue that while Hollywood's industrial logic frames the action cinema, it nonetheless remains a productive critical endeavor to explore the formal commonalities and the broader social significance of action and adventure as genres.

Action: Elements of Genre

So, how should we best make use of concepts of genre to make sense of action and adventure? One strategy is to approach the question historically, as the next chapter aims to do. Another is to identify a set of recurrent themes and formal elements. I've already drawn attention to thematic/narrative elements of conflict, chase and challenge. In trying to pin down the constituent formal elements of the action, it is useful to refine our use of the terms action and adventure, effectively distinguishing between action *sequences* and adventure *narratives*. Action is associated with a particular kind of scene or spectacle (explosions, chases, combat). Adventure, by contrast, implies a story (typically, though not always, the quest narrative) often located within a fantasy or exoticized setting. The search for mythical objects or fabulous treasure in films such as *King Solomon's Mines* (1950) or *Raiders of the Lost Ark* (1981) provide good examples.

While there may be no consistent iconography across the diversity of action and adventure films, set design and special effects – from stop-motion to digital imagery and innovations in 3D – have a privileged place in these genres. Effects are exploited (and in some instances specifically developed) to evoke fantastic worlds and to represent astounding, at times implausible, physical feats. The action movie typically downplays dialogue and complex character development or interaction in favor of spectacular action set-pieces. (Having said this, verbal banter and witty one-liners do play an important part in some action movies.) Indeed it is arguably the case that the emergence of action as a recognized genre descriptor has much to do with such a foregrounding of both visual spectacle and rich sound in blockbuster hits of the 1970s such as *Star Wars*.

Some critics take spectacle to be not only the defining feature of the action blockbuster, but the key to the commercial logic of Hollywood movie-making since this period. Typically this reading is a negative one. In an oft-cited piece screenwriter Larry Gross observes:

> Whatever you call this genre – the movie-as-Theme-park, the movie-as-Giant-Comic-Book, the movie-as-Ride – I call it simply the Big Loud Action Movie. For better or worse it has been a central economic fact, structuring all life, thought and practice in Hollywood at least since the late 70s. This will not change soon. (2000: 3)

For many critics the emergence of the action cinema is cause and symptom of the dominance of the blockbuster, in turn credited with squeezing out smaller more innovative productions despite the evidence that independent productions have thrived in the blockbuster era.

Action films are indeed typically spectacular, they are often expensive to produce and they showcase technology via the very spectacle that defines them. For Gross, the commercial successes of filmmakers Lucas and Spielberg represent a reification of Hollywood's longstanding action tradition. While this argument certainly has purchase, it is worth underlining that not all action and adventure movies are mega-budget affairs deploying cutting edge technology. The development of effective action scenarios through thriller scenarios and suspenseful editing is displayed in an impressive number of lower budget films including the original *The Terminator* (1984) as well as movies made outside Hollywood such as the German arthouse action movie, *Lola Rennt/Run/Lola, Run* (1999) or, decades earlier the trilogy of Italian Westerns directed by Sergio Leone: *A Fistful of Dollars* (1964), *For a Few Dollars More* (1965) and *The Good, the Bad and the Ugly* (1966).

PLATE 1.2 Despite an association with mega-budgets, lower budget action scenarios successfully exploit suspense and editing: Lola's (Franke Potente) exertions organize the action in *Run Lola Run* (1999, directed by Tom Tykwer and produced by X-Filme Creative Pool, Westdeutscher Rundfunk (WDR) and Arte).

While for some it defines Hollywood cinema since the 1980s, spectacle based around movement on screen and rhythmic editing has undoubtedly been an important element, and a central selling point, of American films for decades. Indeed for this reason David Bordwell (2002) talks of "intensified continuity" in his characterization of contemporary film style, emphasizing that features such as rapid editing enhance rather than replace classical technique. The relationship between narrative and spectacle in action cinema has consistently been a topic of critical commentary with several exploring the notion action cinema as ride. Richard Dyer writes with respect to *Speed*: "This is the movie as rollercoaster: all action and next to no plot." Yet Dyer is quick to qualify this statement since, as he makes clear, next to no plot is not the same as no plot at all. Audiences, he observes, typically "want the exhilaration and rush" that such movies offer "embedded in a fiction" (2000: 17). Narrative contextualizes spectacle, giving it meaning as writers such as Geoff King and Lisa Purse have explored in detail. Neither are action sequences or scenes of spectacle simply separable from the narratives in which they appear. They move the narrative along, contributing not only to the tone of the film – excitement, tension and suspense – but to the construction of character.

In *Mission: Impossible,* for example, Ethan Hunt's (Tom Cruise) realization that he is suspected of being a double agent is conveyed in accelerating close ups and dutch angles, culminating in a spectacular explosion that both facilitates his escape and underlines his effective (temporary) separation from the agency for which he works. This combination of speed conveyed via the editing of images that are themselves slowed highlights the visual and thematic juxtapositions so characteristic of action cinema. *Mission: Impossible* exemplifies the 1990s action film in its stylized visual compositions, its generation of excitement and suspense through editing and its use of effects to both slow down and speed up onscreen events. The elements of visual spectacle used here such as exploding glass, points of intense or vivid light against a dark background or the rapid movement of the hero through obstacles, are common within the genre. These devices foreground the particular terrain the hero must navigate in the action film – everyday spaces rendered uncanny sites of violence. In her analysis of the formal qualities of action sequences, Lisa Purse argues that an emphasis on speed, however disorienting visually, is geared towards a theme of mastery of space. She writes that "the thrill of risk is followed by the thrill of mastery," (2011: 63) locating the viewer's experience of both as rooted in the action body.

Sound plays an equally important role in this sequence, just as silence will in a well-known (and much parodied) scene from later in the film in which Hunt is lowered into a vault and must avoid either the slightest sound or increase in temperature that would trigger the alarms. Sound is an aspect of film aesthetic in which action has been at the forefront of innovations from technical developments (THX) to innovative sound designs that extend and deepen visual spectacle. Purse's detailed analysis of action cinema's sound design foregrounds its work in establishing meaning and characterization, noting how different, for example, the exertions of the male and female action hero *sound* in contemporary Hollywood action (2011: 71–75).

Violence and pursuit – the chase – are the two scenarios in which narrative concerns and spectacle most obviously coalesce. These forms allow the elaboration of a number of dynamic patterns: the conflict of hero and villain, the hero pursued and the hero as pursuer. It is likely the preponderance of action sequences that has come to define the genre for contemporary audiences (that is, "action" has to do with both style and content). Arroyo (2000) compares the appearance of action set-pieces to the timing of numbers in the musical, while Lichtenfeld regards the regular timing of action sequences as a formal characteristic of the genre in its modern form. He writes of *Dirty Harry*, the film that for him effectively initiates the modern action movie: "The violence of *Dirty Harry* erupts on a cycle. Each action sequence begins almost exactly ten minutes after the previous one began" (2007: 28).

The analogy often drawn between the action set-piece and the musical number can be understood at a thematic as well as a structural level. That is, action set-pieces play an important role in dramatizing the themes of a movie and drawing audiences in emotionally. In Kathryn Bigelow's war drama *The Hurt Locker* (2008) tense and exhilarating action set-pieces variously convey the bonds between military men, the dangerous conditions in which they work – seen in the abrupt and violent deaths of characters played by Guy Pearce and Ralph Fiennes – and the starkly drawn opposition between the military forces

PLATE 1.3 Violence is both a central theme and pleasure of action: the possibility of violence structures the diverse action sequences of *The Hurt Locker* (2008, directed by Kathryn Bigelow, produced by Voltage Pictures, Grosvenor Park Media, Film Capital Europe Funds (FCEF), First Light Production, Kingsgate Films and Summit Entertainment).

of the United State and the Iraqi citizenry. Along with vivid images of spectacle, the film deploys action sequences of varying pace that achieve different sorts of dramatic effect. They include: a prolonged gun battle in the desert (also staged as a waiting game), race against time sequences in which the team defuse (or, as in the opening sequence, fail to defuse) explosive devices, disorienting chase and urban combat sequences through city streets and buildings, and a drink-fuelled fistfight between comrades. Violence or the threat of violence is thematically central to all of these sequences. As a consequence these action set-pieces centralize themes not only of war but of the body, violence and masculinity (see Atakav and Tasker, 2010). In action movies such sequences involving violence and/or destruction can function as celebrations of physical strength and human agency; but they can equally work to dramatize the limits of the body as individuals are subjected to forces over which they have little or no control. Action is then not an interruption of cinematic story-telling, but part of it.

Action and/or Adventure

"Action" and "adventure" are often used together as terms and are even on occasion treated interchangeably. I've suggested here that, quite apart from whether we think about them as separate genres, we can usefully distinguish between adventure narratives and action sequences: adventure as a kind of story and action as a way of telling stories. Obviously the presence of either an action sequence or an adventure narrative does not in itself mean that an individual film is an example of either the action genre or the adventure cinema. Yet these elements provide starting points. In this book, I argue that the very diversity of the films in which action features as a significant element means that it is most productive to think about action genres. In this way it is possible to keep in view the elements held in common at the same time as we can explore the aesthetic and ideological aspects of the different action types. The book aims to present a range of examples conveying something of the historical development of Hollywood action; it also discusses in detail examples from some of the major action genres and trends in action cinema including war films, urban crime thrillers, espionage and superhero action.

How have scholars approached these questions of definition? In elaborating his definition of historical adventure, Brian Taves seeks to distinguish adventure from action. Action, he writes, is best understood as a "style of storytelling," one which "runs through many genres" and enacts "a male-oriented approach dependent on physical movement, violence and suspense, with often perfunctory motivation and romance" (1993: 5). While there are problems with the designation of a male-oriented approach and the associated idea that some types of film are more appropriate for men and some for women (I take up some of these issues in Chapter 3), Taves' emphasis on energy and movement captures the extent to which action involves a way of handling the narrative and a distinctive set of visual pleasures.

At the other end of the spectrum, Ian Cameron refuses to narrow his study of adventure to "the most obvious adventure movies, the sword-and-bosom epics" suggesting that "[T]he cinema has a facility for turning everything to adventure" (1973: 16). Taves finds this wide-ranging application of the term adventure "so generalized and vague as to be meaningless" (1993: 4). Instead as the starting point for his authoritative study, *The Romance of Adventure,* Taves defines adventure as historical adventure, explicitly excluding fantasy films such as *Raiders of the Lost Ark* since they involve supernatural rather than human agency.

For Taves, in contrast to other action-oriented genres that may be more contemporary, adventure "requires a setting remote in time and space" (1993: 92). Cameron too, although his model of adventure is very different, notes that "the accepted setting is another time and, for most audiences, another place" (1973: 71). Not only is adventure removed from the everyday, it is, both writers concur, a genre defined by a positive emphasis. While he refutes the existence of such a clearly defined entity as the "Adventure Genre," Ian Cameron nonetheless writes of the "positive feeling for adventure" that emerges "both from the exhilaration of the action itself and from the provision of identification figures among the leader characters" (1973). The positive quality of adventure is for these writers in large part connected to the characterization of the hero and his capacity to act positively in the world.

Taking *Robin Hood* as his exemplar of the adventure hero/film, Taves argues that the genre "deals with the valiant fight for freedom and a just form of government, set in exotic locales and the historical past. This is the central theme of adventure, a motif that is unique to the genre" (1993: 4). Differentiating adventure from both action and fantasy, Taves argues for the specificity (and in effect the purity) of historical adventure. Adventure takes place in a space that is temporally and geographically removed, he argues, but not one that is fantastic in character: "Unlike adventure, fantasy presents a netherworld where events violate physical reality and the bounds of human possibility, trespassing the laws of nature and mixing the otherwise separate world of the natural and the supernatural" (1993: 9).

The distinction between the operation of fantasy (with its mystical worlds and magical devices) and adventure films in which the "everyday is replaced by an enlargement of life through imagination" (1993: 12–13) is no doubt a useful one to draw. The impulse to place generic limits around such a potentially diverse body of texts is understandable, and yet *Raiders* feels like an adventure film in the broadest sense of the term. This is not to do with its historical setting, although this is precisely identified. The film is concerned with a quest, with travel and a developing moral sense of the hero's place in the world and his responsibilities to it – all characteristics of adventure. For these reasons, I tend to use adventure in the broader sense that Taves argues against, although in discussing the *Adventures of Robin Hood* (in Chapter 4) I select an example from Taves' more precise category of historical adventure.

In turn, Lichtenfeld argues that action is a genre that emerges with the structures and commercial patterns of New Hollywood. As such he excludes from action the genres – notably the Western and swashbuckler – which he also casts as precursors to modern action. "Obviously," he writes, "the foundation for defining the action movie must be that the films showcase scenes of physical action, be they fistfights, gunfights, swordfights, fights against nature, or other derring-do." (2007: 5) Conceding that there may be an intuitive quality to the criteria, Lichtenfeld too argues that there is a need to draw limits around the category action in order to make it meaningful. The problem in defining both action and adventure then stems from the ubiquitous nature of these sequences, settings and narratives within Hollywood cinema.

Hybrid Genres

Writing on television and genre, Jonathan Bignell summarizes contemporary perspectives on genre when he observes that: "all texts participate in genre to some extent, and often participate in several genres simultaneously" (2008: 117). With its diverse range of settings and styles, such an understanding underpins the analysis of action genres. Altman argues that while reviewers typically seek to pin movies down to particular genres, studio promotion demonstrates a desire to avoid singularity, marketing films via appeals to multiple genres as well as previous successes.[2] Romance features as an element across most genres for example, moderating and interacting with other plotlines whether of adventure, comedy or threat. Once again, this sort of juxtaposition is particularly important for action and adventure since (like romance) both are descriptors most commonly allied to other terms in promotional and reviewing practices.

The films discussed in this book demonstrate that if action *is* a genre – in the most conventional sense of that term, that of a recognizable form of cinema that accrues depth of meaning through the repetition and variation of conventions – it is one that emerges from and participates in any number of allied genres and sub-genres from imperial adventure to science-fiction, to martial arts and war movies. Thus it should be clear that theories of genre hybridity and multiplicity are central to an understanding of action and adventure. Indeed it is no coincidence that critical interest in action and adventure has developed alongside these more flexible models of genre. It might even be argued that critics developed such flexible models in response to the increasingly apparent generic hybridity on display on cinema screens. Altman, for instance, argues that Hollywood films are characterized by "polygeneric strategies," making use of "interlaced narratives characterised by multiple intersections and juxtapositions" (2000: 136). Horror tropes, for example, can be played out in different ways to different effects – in comic, grotesque, effects-led or suspenseful fashion. I don't argue in Chapter 7 that *Pirates of the Caribbean* is a

---

[2] Altman analyzes a series of posters from classical Hollywood movies that make clear the reluctance to "explicitly [identify] a film with a single genre" (2000: 57).

horror movie, but I do suggest that it draws on the sort of effects and imagery exploited in an earlier blockbuster horror action hybrid, *The Mummy* (1999). *Pirates* stages a particular intersection of swashbuckling adventure with horror and romance; making sense of the movie in generic terms means acknowledging those connections rather than erasing them in favor of the designation action-adventure. Similarly, *Rambo: First Blood Part II,* discussed in Chapter 8, is a defining 1980s action film. Yet, as various critics have acknowledged, it also clearly incorporates elements from war movies, jungle adventure and POW narratives. Altman's observation that, "not all genre films relate to their genre in the same way or to the same extent" (2000: 221), is surely relevant here.

Another way of thinking about these questions of genre hybridity and the diverse movies in which action plays an important part, is to talk about action as a mode as well as a genre. As a mode action has as much to with a way of telling a story – or perhaps more exactly visualizing that story – as the *kind* of stories that are told. Both action sequences and action films emphasize the dynamism of the moving image, whether that is expressed via movement within the frame or an accelerated pace of editing. Music and sound play an important – and relatively underexplored – part in the action sequence/film, anticipating and complementing the sense of urgency expressed through character and vehicle movement. Such an emphasis on speed, conflict and movement is routinely juxtaposed with an aesthetic that celebrates scale, one that invites viewers to contemplate – even immerse themselves in – the effects, sets and spectacular scenes.

CHAPTER 2

ACTION AND ADVENTURE: HISTORICAL AND CULTURAL OVERVIEW

By the 1980s, the term "action" was routinely used in promotion and reviewing practices with action and adventure movies increasingly dominating the box office. While it is tempting therefore to regard this as the genre's point of origin, throughout its history, action, adventure and spectacle have been pronounced features of Hollywood cinema. Richard Slotkin observes that action is effectively "an extrapolation of the most essential narrative elements from all of the pre-existing action-oriented genres: Western, combat film, horror movie, crime film science-fiction" (Lichtenfeld, 2007: xi). Today, action is both a distinctive genre and a hybrid form of story-telling that is applied to a diverse range of contents. Action encompasses the apocalyptic science-fiction scenario of *Armageddon* (1998), the future world

The Hollywood Action and Adventure Film, First Edition. Yvonne Tasker.
© 2015 John Wiley & Sons, Inc. Published 2015 by John Wiley & Sons, Inc.

PLATE 2.1 Contemporary action encompasses diverse and hybrid forms: both Hollywood and British, *Skyfall* couples revenge themes with espionage (2012, directed by Sam Mendes and produced by Eon Productions, Danjaq and B23).

spectacle of violent combat in *The Hunger Games* (2012) and a tale of revenge and espionage in *Skyfall* (2012).

This chapter briefly maps the historical development of action and adventure in Hollywood cinema highlighting some of the important shifts and briefly placing these in industrial and cultural context. It also identifies points of continuity and repetition, delineating cycles and trends within the broad generic spaces of action and adventure. I take this approach since, while it is tempting to articulate an evolutionary model of action and adventure cinema – progressively more sophisticated and self-conscious – this can obscure as much as it reveals. As discussed in the previous chapter, while traditions of action adventure filmmaking have long roots in Hollywood they are also characterized by a high degree of diversity. Moreover, the genre's marked association with patterns of recycled culture tends to undercut an evolutionary chronology – whether this is conducted as parody in films such as *Last Action Hero* (1993), as pastiche, as in *Star Wars*, or in earnest, as in *Dirty Harry*'s visual and thematic debt to the Western. The overview takes a broadly chronological approach, commencing with the identification of action and adventure as key components of early and silent cinemas.

Cut to the Chase: Action in Early and Silent Cinema

At a relatively early stage of film history, elements of chase and pursuit were developed into basic narratives through innovations in editing, evident in such cinematic reference points as *Daring Daylight Burglary* (1903), a "fast-paced crime thriller" in the United Kingdom or *The Great Train Robbery* (1903) in the United States. *The Great Train Robbery* is often discussed as a point of origin for the Western, while *Daring Daylight Burglary* (said to have influenced Porter's film) demonstrates the longevity of crime and violence as a narrative frame for the chase. Both titles involve crime, some form of pursuit and the ultimate capture of the thieves in question by the forces of law. The sensational appeals of crime and pursuit (and indeed war and conflict) remain evident throughout the silent period. Film historians such as Richard Abel (2004) and Ben Singer (2001) have done much to map the appeals of sensational cinema in the period, pointing out that what we now typically term "action" was framed within the silent era as a form of popular melodrama featuring scenes of peril, pursuit, villainy and rescue, forms derived in part from spectacular theatrical traditions. These basic elements of chase and pursuit were also given comic inflection in Mack Sennett's highly successful slapstick Keystone productions, most notably through the antics of the "Keystone Kops" in numerous films from 1912 to 1917. The rudimentary yet highly entertaining – and lucrative – character of these chase narratives is suggestive for the future development of the genre. Gerald Mast captures the absurd and exhilarating visual gags in Sennett's *Lizzies of the Field* (1924) in which "autos fly through the air, crash into each other, carom in impossible patterns, extend themselves in space, scoop up passersby, and collapse in heaps of rubble – all the while appearing to travel at 100 miles per hour" (1979: 57). Chase and pursuit scenarios were from the earliest days inflected in both thrilling and comic directions. Tico Romao's (2004) analysis of the car chase as a feature of 1960s and 1970s action, examines a history of representation in which pursuit sequences showcased new techniques and location work and the multiple ways in which the car had come to signify youth, rebellion and danger in American culture of the period.

Film historians have also drawn attention to the surprisingly central place occupied by women in early action and adventure scenarios, a prominence understood in terms of contemporary discourses of the "New Woman." As Singer writes, the serial queen melodramas that achieved significant commercial success in the Teens – Pearl White's *The Perils of Pauline* and *The Exploits of Elaine* (both 1914) made her one of the top box office draws of the time – were characterized by an "extraordinary emphasis on female heroism." Singer summarizes:

> Within a sensational action–adventure framework of the sort generally associated with male heroics, serials gave narrative pre-eminence to an intrepid young heroine who exhibited a variety of traditionally "masculine" qualities: physical strength and endurance, self-reliance, courage, social authority, and freedom to explore novel experiences outside the domestic. (2001: 221)

Such portrayals of female heroism seem "extraordinary" not only in the context of the period since the sort of action heroine who appeared in, for example, 1970s television (*Charlie's Angels* [1976–1981, *Wonder Woman* [1975–1979]) or 2000s Hollywood (*Lara Croft: Tomb Raider* [2001] and its sequel *The Cradle of Life* [2003]) tends to be imagined as entirely new. As students of women's history will know, the "New Woman" appears cyclically at moments of societal change – albeit with different designators. So too do the sorts of thrilling action and adventure scenarios in which she features.

Sensation, melodrama and modernity are all key terms here. As Singer and writers such as Steve Neale have noted, action and adventure scenarios flourished during the teens and twenties, understood partly in terms of their origins in theatrical melodrama. Indeed Neale notes that the Fairbanks film *The Gaucho* (1927) was described by *Film Daily* as action–adventure (1999: 55). Sensational melodrama of the kind Singer explores incorporate sensation scenes such as fights, leaps from building, escape from danger or the aversion of disaster "just in time." These sensation scenes perform similar functions to contemporary action set-pieces, the accelerating scope and scale of which have been considered to define the emergence of the genre.

Both Singer and Jennifer Bean frame such an emphasis on sensation in terms of modernity, both in terms of the technology required to stage/film such scenes and in the "context of modern hyperstimulus" (Singer, 2001: 12) that gives rise to them. Bean notes that the *Hazards of Helen* serials (1914–1917) repeatedly present scenarios in which technology is both vital and unreliable, characterized by "treacherous instability" (2004: 22). Such tropes would continue to play a central role in action and adventure films, both in the chaos caused by machinery gone wrong (*Speed* [1994], *Unstoppable* [2010]), and in the generations of heroes and heroines who make use of technology in innovative and unexpected ways (e.g., the loader with which Ripley (Sigourney Weaver) defeats the mother alien in *Aliens* [1986]). Just as often the action hero sets technology aside in favor of more seemingly authentic and unmediated forms of action. In other words s/he is associated with, but not limited by, the dependence on machinery that defines modernity.

As Bean's comments on the serial and sensational melodrama suggest, the silent period also sees the development of a clear association between action-adventure filmmaking and techniques designed to deliver spectacle; special and visual effects would continue to be important aspects of the genre. Indeed in industrial terms action and adventure cinemas are very much associated with formal and techno-logical innovations designed to achieve particular effects: from the use of editing to generate suspense, to the use of stop-motion animation and other techniques to convey menacing or fantastic worlds, from the development of techniques to safely deliver convincing chase scenarios involving cars, trains and other forms of transport to the steadicam that enabled films to convey the speed of the chase in new ways.

The appeal of films such as the Jules Verne adaptation *20,000 Leagues Under the Sea* (1916), involved not only the adaptation of a hugely popular book, but elaborate underwater sequences.[1] Willis O'Brien's ground-breaking stop-motion animation detailing dinosaurs in the lavish 1925 adaptation of Sir Arthur Conan Doyle's *The Lost World* is another significant achievement. *The Lost World* is a landmark of effects-led adventure cinema, involving elaborate scenes of jungle adventure, spectacular battles between dinosaurs coupled with the human actors as awestruck witnesses. The titles include informative commentary as when an Allosaurus ("the most vicious pest of the ancient world" pro-nounces Challenger) tackles a Triceratops defending its young. The dramatic scene of an exploding volcano that sets the jungle ablaze

[1]   Verne's novel was first published in 1870.

features both humans and dinosaurs fleeing. Such laboriously produced films – the trailer for *The Lost World* proclaimed that it had been seven years in production – which exploited and developed a variety of technical innovations indicate the early importance of spectacular scenes as a defining feature of action and adventure cinema, and the association of the genre with technological advances.

The bullet-time deployed in *The Matrix* (1999) or James Cameron's *Avatar* (2009) with its innovative use of specifically developed technology, provide more contemporary reference points. What links these films of different eras is an – at times contradictory – impulse to produce cinematic spectacle that draws attention to the work of the film, that *makes us see* and admire the image, and to convey an impression of fantastic actions or spaces in a manner that is at least plausible and at best immersive for the spectator. On this score the genre's association with technological innovation is not the only production dimension we might note. The fabulous sets of the Douglas Fairbanks adventures represent a distinct source of spectacle in the adventure tradition of the silent Hollywood cinema. *Robin Hood* (1922), with its pageantry and

PLATE 2.2 Innovations in special effects have been central to the thematic and visual impact of adventure cinema: here a brontosaurus rampages through London in *The Lost World* (1925, directed by Harry O. Hoyt and produced by First National Pictures).

battle scenes, poetic recreation of castles and vast cast cost $1.5 million to produce, setting a record at that time (Balio, 1993: 205).

The jungle adventure cycle that *The Lost World* arguably initiated was coupled with sensational horror in the later and equally effects-oriented early sound film *King Kong* (1933) both of which allowed O'Brien to innovate in stop-motion animation.[2] Both films stage sensational conflicts between humans and a fantastical natural world with scenes of peril and pursuit. In *The Lost World*, for example, Professor Challenger (Wallace Beery) and his team travel through the Amazonian jungle into a fantastical land inhabited by dinosaurs, the original trailer promising audiences "The Greatest Attraction your eyes have ever beheld." A newspaper headline (rather than a conventional inter-title) tells us that the explorers have reached the "last outpost of civilization" and that they are about to head into a "Mystery World via Secret Rivers." In the film's climactic scenes a brontosaurus rampages through the City of London before collapsing Tower Bridge and swimming away to Challenger's dismay. The sequence stages a familiar generic theme in which untamed/disruptive elements of the wild are introduced into the complex urban space, juxtaposing modernity with primitivism. In her study of *King Kong*, Cynthia Erb notes the salience of the combined conventions of "the travel documentary and jungle adventure traditions" (1998: 66) for making sense of the film. As Erb notes, jungle adventure shares with the Western a use of natural imagery to define the limits and the virtues of modernity. Thus, "Thirties jungle films frequently alternate between demonic and edenic images." (1998: 92).

The best known articulations of jungle adventure are elaborated around the figure of Tarzan, introduced in Edgar Rice Burroughs' novel *Tarzan of the Apes* in 1912. While this began in the silent cinema with Elmo Lincoln in the title role of *Tarzan of the Apes* (1918), but more significant commercially and undoubtedly better known is the MGM series of films featuring Olympian Johnny Weissmuller in the title role (the first of these released in 1932 was hugely successful).

---

[2] In literary terms *King Solomon's Mines* is said to have initiated the adventure plot of a lost world, influencing writers such as Conan Doyle. Although Haggard's novel was a best seller on its publication in 1885, it was not adapted for the screen until the British production of 1937.

These sound era films underlined the fascination with the presence of white Westerners in jungle spaces understood as primitive. Such scenarios are clearly framed and inflected by colonialist discourses, racial hierarchies and the pleasures of both exotic and erotic spectacle (the two are frequently conflated). While, as Erb notes, a film like *King Kong* drew on the producers associations with ethnographic and documentary film, the jungle adventure tradition coupled stock footage with studio work and suitably accessible locations. In *Tarzan the Ape Man*, location work took place across a number of American settings – largely California – which, along with stock footage, stood in for Africa. In these instances and in jungle and other adventure films produced in subsequent decades an idea of the travelogue's allure, of settings as romantic spaces of possibility (where the location itself is neither specified nor authentic) informs promotional appeal.

Action and Adventure in the Studio Era

Within the classical or studio era of Hollywood filmmaking a variety of action and adventure types were produced, several achieving distinct generic status: the Western, gangster and war film most pre-eminently, but also as mentioned in the previous section jungle adventure. Indeed a comment attributed to Errol Flynn – "Robin Hood and his men were sort of twelfth century Tarzans" (Wallace, 1938: 28) – connects *The Adventures of Robin Hood* to that tradition. Given that these familiar action-based genres are each in their own right formally and thematically complex and have generated significant amounts of scholarship, while noting connections with these genres here I focus primarily on the historical adventure film as one of the studio era's chief manifestations of action and adventure. Additionally, I identify the action and adventure components of these well-known genres.

The Western, as detailed previously, emerges in the early cinema with the chase scenario enacted in *The Great Train Robbery* typically regarded as formative. Like jungle adventure, Westerns frequently foreground conflict with and within a natural setting that is both enchantingly beautiful and yet dangerous. Contestations between heroes and outlaws, settlers and Native Americans each stage differently themes of colonial hierarchy and the establishment of law and order. As Robert

Warshow observes, "men with guns" provide a common element between the Western and gangster genres: "Guns as physical objects, and the postures associated with their use, form the visual and emotional centre of both types of films" (1964: 89). Although he is inclined to see this as ultimately a rather superficial connection, Warshow eloquently elaborates the ways in which weaponry suggest "continually the possibility of violence" (1964, 93). Not only the urban environment, but also the gangster's criminality – which necessitates his death – differentiates the violence in these genres. Scenes of violent confrontation provide sensational set-pieces in both: guns fired from moving cars, the gangster's death in the gangster film, and the ritualized gunfight in the Western town. An emphasis on speed and movement – cars, galloping horses, the heroes speed of response in scenes of conflict – remain familiar action elements.[3]

Like the Western, the war film has its origins in the silent period with seminal titles such as *What Price Glory?* (1926). However, it is in films of and about World War II that the war film as a genre developed many of the conventions we recognize today. In terms of the historical development of action and adventure cinema, both the fact of war experienced by audiences and the film industry's willingness to offer patriotic fare with an action emphasis are significant factors. The war film's presentation of heroes who are impelled towards violence by duty as much as character, as well as the articulation of emotionally intense bonds between comrades under fire, are recognizable components of contemporary action cinema. Moreover, like the Western the war film has the potential to convey moral ambiguity in relation to its representation of violence, to take note of what is lost as well as to celebrate the excitement of action.[4] The significance of the war film for action is addressed in more detail in Chapter 5.

[3] Warshow writes that while even the gangster's leisure is "compulsively aggressive," he is nonetheless "graceful, moving like a dancer among the crowded dangers of the city." Such an evocation of choreography and grace chimes with the emphasis on mobility and with the connections critics have routinely drawn between action and the musical in recent years (1964: 89–90).
[4] Warshow holds a different view, suggesting that the war movie is "continually marred by ideological sentimentality" and lacks the "drama of self-restraint" staged by the Western with the hero's capacity for violent action (1964: 105).

Historical adventure films also foreground violence and conflict, albeit in a less intense manner. Like the Western they are typically set in the past, though not necessarily an American past. Once again classical historical adventure builds on the spectacular films produced in the silent era, notably the films of Douglas Fairbanks such as *The Mark of Zorro* (1920) or *The Black Pirate* (1926). Despite the commercial significance of studio-era historical adventure, often among the most prestigious productions of their day, the genre remains relatively underdeveloped within genre criticism. Working within an industrial rather than a genre studies framework, Balio explores the production trend of "costume-adventure films" that achieved commercial success in the 1930s. Though by no means associated with one studio alone, Warner Brothers notably generated a series of successful historical adventures featuring Errol Flynn, first as the eponymous hero in *Captain Blood* (1935) and subsequently in titles such as *The Charge of the Light Brigade* (1936). Flynn was once more paired with female lead Olivia De Havilland in the commercial and critical success that is discussed in Chapter 4, *The Adventures of Robin Hood* (1938), a film that, with its spectacular sets and scenes of combat, built on the Fairbanks successes of the silent period. Flynn's films for Warner's demonstrate the diverse settings that swashbuckling historical adventure employed, from pirate adventures to war stories and "Merrie England." Across such films the past provides a colorful setting for adventure, stylized combat and romance.

The historical adventure continued as a Hollywood staple through the mid-1950s, showcasing various athletic, pin-up male stars including Tyrone Power, Douglas Fairbanks Jr, Burt Lancaster and Stewart Granger. The independently produced *The Crimson Pirate* (1958) exemplifies many of the adventure films elements in this era: playful tone, a spectacular star (Lancaster) who gives an athletic performance, comedy scenes (including one in which Lancaster and sidekick Nick Cravat appear in drag), sea battles and a populist-themed narrative that sets in opposition the physicality and freedom of the pirate/outlaw and the restrictive forces of the state.

In contrast to the serial queens of the silent era, women in adventure films may be feisty, even rebellious, but their capacity for violence or action is significantly curtailed and is largely subsumed into their

PLATE 2.3 Historical adventure cinema coupled spectacle and humor. Vallo (Burt Lancaster) addresses the cinema audience in *The Crimson Pirate* (1958, directed by Robert Siodmak and produced by Hecht-Lancaster Productions).

romantic function for the hero. Taves suggests that the terms of historical adventure's commitment to period realism means that female characters are frequently marginalized. However, he also notes that these genres codes do not by definition exclude women from taking an active role and that the genre's ideological commitment to ideas of liberty should surely make it a good space for this to happen. He writes: "Although women are often isolated in a subordinate status, those who are brave may become heroes in their own right. Enjoying the same life-style, these female counterparts break through feminine stereotypes to prove their own courage and daring" (1993: 130). If an involvement in action sequences – an ability to fight and the presentation of that ability as a source of spectacle – defines the genre, then women in the classical era are particularly confined even though they are clearly present.

Imperial themed adventure continues with greater emphasis if anything on location shooting. The 1950 box office hit *King Solomon's Mines* (one of several adaptations of Rider Haggard's novel) was shot in Africa, encountering considerable difficulties including shooting in temperatures of 150 degrees Fahrenheit, serious illness among the crew and star Deborah Kerr collapsing. A telegram from producer Sam Zimbalist to director Compton Bennett acknowledges the difficulties faced but insists on the importance of location shooting: "Appreciate all difficulties you are having but under no circumstances consider shooting unfriendly village at studio." Bennett is urged to use "Turkana or any other colourful tribe but please do not over-dress or over-paint natives to make them unreal." Additionally the telegram warns that "We are in great danger of picture fiasco due to lack of sufficient animal thrills and African color."[5] Another telegram urged that "tempo must be increased and maintained," signaling the need to balance action with the spectacle of African scenes. This contradictory emphasis on realism and the need for color characterizes the discourse at work here, marked by a desire to reveal Africa to American viewers in a manner that can be termed realist, in turn measured by the perceived need to conform to the exoticism and excitement provided by the adventure film. Thus the trailer proclaims the film to be, "Actually filmed in the savage heart of equatorial Africa." Although the novel's plotline around Umbopa's status as rightful ruler of the hidden lands remains, native peoples form the backdrop to this action, effectively serving as a component of the scenery.

During the 1960s epic fantasy films such as *Jason and the Argonauts* (1963) coupled the set-pieces and fantastic worlds of historical adventure with a renewed emphasis on special effects. The film's climactic scene displayed the heroes battling seven skeletons that emerge from the ground armed with shields and swords. In turn the swashbuckling tradition was revived in the 1970s, with films such as the US/UK production of *The Three Musketeers* (1973). By this point historical adventure had become firmly associated with a comic – even camp – tone that informed later examples of recycled adventure such as *Raiders of the Lost Ark*, *The Mummy* and *Pirates of the Caribbean*. Nonetheless, it would be wrong to argue that historical adventure had entirely shifted towards comedy or parody – the implication of an evolutionary model of genre – since films such as Ridley Scott's *Gladiator* (2000) and his

5   Telegram from Sam Zimbalist, November 22 1949 to Compton Bennett in Nairobi, Rudy Behlmer papers, Margaret Herrick Library.

later *Kingdom of Heaven* (2005) are epic action dramas played straight-forwardly in line with, rather than against, the genre employing the setting of the Roman Empire and the Crusades respectively.

World War II and Post-War Action

Unsurprisingly, World War II involved significant shifts in the development of what we now call the Hollywood action film. The intensification of the war movie itself, and the refinement of the World War II combat film, as detailed by Jeanine Basinger, is the most obvious aspect of that process. This period also sees the emergence of what critics will retrospectively term "*film noir*," a mode of filmmaking that Lichtenfeld sees as informing the emergence of contemporary action traditions in American cinema. *Film noir* is itself a contested category; notoriously leaky as a genre it is just as often understood as a style that imparts an atmosphere of menace and moral ambiguity. If *noir* as a style is aligned with any particular generic marker it is the thriller, and it is the connections between the sensational and thrilling components of the action film that I wish to draw attention to here. The *noir* style works to build suspense, excitement and a suggestion of menace along with, importantly, the potential for violence to erupt at any moment.

Both the war film and *noir* involve a franker engagement with violence and death than previous Hollywood genres had typically allowed. The cynicism – or, for some, nihilism – that characterizes much *film noir* also registers in some war movies albeit rather later, with films that qualify the more patriotic/heroic register of the war film not appearing until the 1960s. Just as significantly the 1940s cycle of *noir* deploys either explicitly or implicitly the figure of the male veteran, a man whose experience of violence in some ways render him damaged and unsuitable for the civilian world. Two elements in particular are worth noting in terms of the development of American action and adventure: firstly the damaged veteran as a heroic type and the figuring of violent masculinity more generally; secondly the articulation of themes to do with race and ethnicity as significant elements of American identity.

World War II films emphasize ordinary men's capacity for violence; the films depict a military that mixes conscripts with professional soldiers, units made up of men who have civilian lives and loved ones to which they long to return. The violent experience of war promotes bonds between men, but also raises questions about the lives they will lead once war is over (obviously films made during WWII are different in some respect from those made after, although following the end of World War II in 1945, the United States became embroiled in the Korean War between 1950 and 1953). *Marine Raiders* (1944) openly debates the viability of romantic attachments in time of war. The opening scenes vividly depict action; the hero, traumatized by what he has seen, then forms a romantic attachment with a military woman who also plays her part. As in the Western romance serves to suggest connectedness to a community ensuring the hero is not subsumed by bitterness. The figure of the returning/damaged veteran who is fundamentally asocial is centrally inscribed in 1980s Hollywood action in the figure of John Rambo (Sylvester Stallone). Early critics identifying *film noir* as a distinct style in the immediate post-war years were clearly aware of the context of war. Paul Schrader would spell this out in his essay "Notes on *Film Noir*" in which he argued for an "immediate post-war disillusionment," a disappointment with American society "directly mirrored in the sordidness of the urban crime film" (1972: 10).

Though Schrader does not address this, tensions around race and citizenship were significant aspect of the post-war period in American society albeit rarely registering in cinema. Action and adventure is a generic tradition within which questions of race and ethnicity play an important part, as I'll argue throughout this book. In a rather different way than the Western – which is underwritten by racial hierarchies of settlers and native Americans – themes of race and ethnicity are central components of both war and *noir* films. War films of course mobilize crude constructions of the ethnic other in their presentation of the enemy; from the Japanese of World War II films through the portrayal of Vietnamese forces to the Iraqi insurgents of twenty-first century war movies. While there may be specificity to the particular stereotypes deployed in movies featuring these conflicts, they all share an emphasis on primitivism, simplicity and brutality. Yet as Basinger shows, World War II films were required to negotiate American hierarchies of race and ethnicity in a more complex manner. In wartime both Hollywood and the government mobilized a rhetoric of unity and democracy – fighting for freedom – which was plainly at odds with the racial hierarchies and inequalities of American society. The US military was racially segregated until 1948, but Basinger shows the World War II combat film evolved a format that allowed it to evoke America as an inclusive, cooperative force bringing together individuals from different ethnic backgrounds. African-American quarterback Jim Brown's role in *The Dirty Dozen* (1967) was significant in part since it contested decades of marginalizing black military experience within Hollywood cinema. Brown's physical power and speed is fully on display, placing his character as central to the action most spectacularly in the climactic scene in which he runs, cheered by the remaining members of the Dozen, dropping grenades down the air vents of a Chateaux in which the German high command and their female companions have been imprisoned. This heroic atrocity is the culmination of the Dozen's "unholy teamwork," as Basinger puts it, both a bitter commentary on and an exciting staging of violence.

Action and Adventure in the "New Hollywood"

With the gradual demise of the production code and the introduction of a ratings system in 1968, Hollywood films of the 1970s begin to push acceptable boundaries with respect to screen violence. A clearly

PLATE 2.4 Jim Brown's role in *The Dirty Dozen* contested Hollywood's marginalization of African-American experience in war movies (1967, directed by Robert Aldrich and produced by Metro-Goldwyn-Mayer (MGM), MKH and Seven Arts Productions).

differentiated, adult form of violent cinema emerges in which scenes of dramatic and bloody death are vividly portrayed. For many, this is the beginning of a recognizable action cinema in the contemporary sense of that term. Films such as *The Dirty Dozen*, *Bonnie and Clyde* (1967), *The Wild Bunch* (1969) and *The French Connection* (1971) presented violence and speed in direct and novel ways. Tico Romao points to the distinctive quality achieved in *Bullitt* (1968)'s car chase sequences by shooting actors in actual moving vehicles rather using rear screen projection in the studio; contrasting the credibility of the scenes in *Bullitt* with those used in the previous year's *Bonnie and Clyde*, Romao links this technique with a wider move to revitalize the police thriller via a realist aesthetic (2004: 130–134). The series of films initiated by Don Siegel's *Dirty Harry* (1971), featuring Clint Eastwood as the eponymous rogue cop, routinely feature shocking images of death, violence and torture. On its release the film triggered intense debate regarding the politics of film violence as well as the relationship between Hollywood cinema and on-going debates around policing.

During the 1960s and 1970s familiar genres underwent redefinition, whether in pursuit of audiences or in a spirit of aesthetic innovation. While many critics have identified the revisionist Western as a significant feature of these decades, a comparable revisionism is also at work across a number of genres, including the war film. The involvement of the United States in the Korean and Vietnam Wars (and the media coverage of these conflicts) is clearly a factor in these developments. The emergence of the dirty war movie, which seemed to question the nobility or heroism of combat while staging spectacular combat/action sequences, pushed the barriers of censorship with respect to the representation of violence.

The exemplary dirty war movie is *The Dirty Dozen*, directed by Robert Aldrich Famously condemned by *New York Times* film critic Bosley Crowther, *The Dirty Dozen* featured a new generation of male stars. Crowther condemned both film and audience when he wrote of the film's "blatant and obvious appeal to the latent aggressiveness and sadism in undiscriminating viewers." For Tony Williams, Crowther's condemnation of the film and, in the original piece, of Sergio Leone's *For a Few Dollars More* (1965) ("as socially decadent and dangerous as LSD"), suggests "unease with both changing times and new depictions of screen violence" (2004: 346). What characterizes both *The Dirty Dozen* and Leone's *Dollar* films is a disinterest in reverence for genre conventions or for the hierarchies of authority or virtue that they typically involved. The protagonists are cynical and amoral – criminals in the *Dozen*, a bounty hunter in the *Dollar* films.

Dirty Dozen director Robert Aldrich remarked that he found the original script "old-fashioned" adding, "I don't think that a 1945 war picture is necessarily a good 1967 war picture" (Arnold and Miller, 1986: 124). As Williams notes, it was *Bonnie and Clyde*, released the same year as *The Dirty Dozen* and also scathingly reviewed by Crowther, which has achieved critical recognition. *Bonnie and Clyde* is celebrated for its particular take on the conventional death of the gangster that closes the film. The central characters are blown apart by a hail of bullets; shot with multiple cameras, bodily destruction is rendered graphic and immediate.

Informed in a rather different way by anti-establishment culture and politics, the 1960s and 1970s saw the emergence of a cycle of thrillers in which the protagonist is caught up within a bewildering and extensive conspiracy. Paranoid traditions continue well into the 1970s with critics typically framing this tradition in terms of popular skepticism towards official government in the wake of the Watergate scandal and the US military involvement in Vietnam. Films such as *The Manchurian Candidate* (1962) and *Seven Days in May* (1964) are tense political/military thrillers featuring set-piece action sequences. If these and later conspiracy narratives such as *The Conversation* seem grounded in the political contexts of the period, they nonetheless pick up on longstanding populist themes in American culture that are particularly suited to an action-oriented mode of narration. The individual is pitted against corrupt authority, engaged in a race against time. More recent surveillance or persecution fantasies, such as *Enemy of the State* (1998), the futuristic *Minority Report* (2002) or *I, Robot* (2004) and *The Bourne Identity* (2002) suggest the more general appeal of these themes across historical periods. All involve sequences depicting the hero fleeing for his life, an imagery that suggests his mastery or space as much as the threats he faces.

The 1970s also saw the emergence of a distinct black action cinema (sometimes discussed under the banner of "Blaxploitation") with both male and female heroes deploying violence, gun power and martial arts skills against oppressive enemies and institutions. Both independently produced and studio forms of black action cinema emerged in this period, the latter exemplified by *Shaft* (1971), starring Richard Roundtree as a tough private investigator in the urban action mode. As I develop in the next chapter (Chapter 3), critical perspectives on Blaxploitation are indicative of ambivalent responses to action more generally as well as suspicion of Hollywood's frequently clumsy efforts to attract young African-American audiences. While this mode of film production effectively recognized black audiences and gave welcome roles to black performers, action has frequently traded in familiar but unwelcome racial and sexual stereotypes that audiences must negotiate.

In terms of mainstream Hollywood productions, African-American characters have frequently occupied supporting rather than starring roles, although this is not to say they are thus excluded from action. From Danny Glover's older partner role in the *Lethal Weapon* (1987) films to Laurence Fishburne's philosophically inclined mentor and sparring partner, Morpheus, in *The Matrix* (1999) African-American men have taken high profile action roles. The successes of Eddie Murphy's action-comedy *Beverly Hills Cop* (1984), Denzel Washington's action-thriller roles (such as *Man on Fire* [2004]) and Will Smith's prominence as an action star following the massive success of *Independence Day* (1996) suggested something of a shift. Smith has starred primarily in action films that exploit his comic style – notably the *Men in Black* series (1997, 2002, 2012) in which he plays the bemused hero to Tommy Lee Jones' stone-faced partner – although he tackles non-comic action roles in *Enemy of the State* and *I, Robot*.

Independence Day exemplifies another important dimension of the "new Hollywood" that impacts on action and adventure – the increased significance of the blockbuster and its associated release strategies. Since the late 1970s, action and adventure has become synonymous with some of the most costly, highly promoted and profitable Hollywood films and franchises. The blockbuster incarnation of action and adventure in this period makes clear its debts to earlier periods of Hollywood history as well as its association with sequels and cycles. While action and adventure forms took on challenging material (in terms of both censorship and mainstream taste) in the

1970s, the end of that decade saw the emergence of an adventure tradition geared to younger/family audiences. The release of George Lucas' enormously successful fantasy adventure *Star Wars* underlined the commercial potential of "safe" adventure scenarios. Lucas and contemporary Steven Spielberg – director of adventure hits such as *Raiders of the Lost Ark* (which Lucas produced) and *Jurassic Park* (1993) – have come to represent a commercially lucrative yet culturally conservative version of the action-adventure film, one which remains very much in evidence as apparent in the *Lord of the Rings* films (2001, 2002, 2003) and in adaptations of children's fiction such as the Harry Potter films. I look at *Raiders* in more detail in Chapter 7, placing it alongside *Pirates of the Caribbean* as a more recent example of recycled film culture. These adventure films look back to some of the Hollywood traditions outlined earlier in this chapter – chase sequences, exotic settings and extensive effects work. They also typically reaffirm the ethnic and racial hierarchies of the adventure tradition.

The prominence of adventure formats in contemporary action is bound up not only in an aesthetic of recycled culture but an industry that is seeking to develop its audience. Lichtenfeld points to a trend by which action is "aging down" in a quest for larger audiences, interacting with the family film (and the marketing category of family adventure). Disney is of course, as he notes, a key player in this process. He writes:

> While films like the *Pirates of the Caribbean* and *National Treasure* might not have been considered 'action' films in previous decades, they have gained much ground in earning that designation, largely because the action genre has become an increasingly amorphous class of pictures. (2007: 322)

Peter Krämer situates this trend in the late 1970s. He writes that "most of Hollywood's superhits since 1977 are basically, like *Star Wars*, children's films; more precisely, they are children's films for the whole family, and for teenagers, too" (2004: 366). While the adult-oriented action that achieved box office success in the 1980s – discussed in relation to *Die Hard* and *Rambo: First Blood Part II* in Chapter 8 but evident in more recent films such as *Crank* (2006) – runs counter to this argument, the trend is nonetheless significant.

Action Cinema: Violence, Spectacle

If Spielberg and Lucas became synonymous with the commercial potential of adventure from the late 1970s onwards, in the 1980s "action" came to suggest rather different – if related – cinematic qualities. Action became a widely used term in promotion and reviewing to signal films as generic, rather than describing one element of a film's repertoire of pleasures or a type of sequence. Violent, cynical though tempered by an admittedly bleak humor, the 1980s saw the appearance of high profile and hugely successful action franchises. These include the Vietnam veteran focused Rambo films, the rogue cop *Lethal Weapon* (1987, 1989, 1992, 1998), *Die Hard* (1988, 1990, 1995, 200, 2013), as well as the science-fiction and horror action franchises of the *Alien* (1979, 1986, 1992, 1997), *Terminator* (1984, 1991, 2003, 2009) and *Robocop* (1987, 1990, 1993) films. In different ways these 1980s action films foregrounded an aesthetic of violence that centered the body in distinctive ways. The interface between action, science-fiction and horror, for example, generates spectacles of bodies that are torn apart (*Alien*), reconstructed (*Robocop*) or synthetic (Schwarzenegger as relentless cyborg). While it is tempting to collapse these films together, writers such as Lichtenfeld have shown how the genre shifts in significant ways through the decade. For example, Lichtenfeld notes the impact of *Die Hard*'s commercial success, that film effectively triggering a vogue in everyman, never-say-die heroic figures moving away from the early-mid 1980s trend towards hyperbolic, muscular male stars.

While 1980s action was for many associated with an articulation of specifically male violence, with built male bodies dominating screens, action films of this period also incorporated female performers in tough action roles both supporting and in some instances as action protagonist. Sigourney Weaver's metamorphosis from sole survivor of *Alien* to the aggressive and capable figure she plays in *Aliens* exemplifies what contemporary critics regarded as a gender shift with both films widely discussed. The muscular body and heroic yet troubled role of Linda Hamilton as Sarah Connor in the 1991 hit *Terminator 2: Judgment Day* (like *Aliens*, directed by James Cameron) also attracted equal attention. As we've seen, however, Hollywood's positioning of women in adventure scenarios is by no means new. Throughout its Hollywood history, an undoubtedly male-dominated genre has nonetheless featured action and adventure movies either centered on women or featuring women in tough supporting roles. What drew critics to these 1980s and early 1990s movies then was a female articulation of the latest action cycle, one foregrounding personal cynicism, toughness and the body.

Action and comedy, a feature of some 1980s films, became an increasingly common pairing in the 1990s, as darker action narratives gave way to more or less explicit action-comedy and tongue in cheek enactments of the genre's conventions and character types. This lighter generic tone allowed the play with gender to continue, albeit in ways that typically remained conventionally hierarchical. Cameron's *True Lies* (1994) enacts a comic – yet bleakly violent – action scenario in which Jamie Lee Curtis is drawn into husband Schwarzenegger's secret world of espionage and adventure. The Shane Black-scripted *The Long Kiss Goodnight* (1996) also features both tongue-in-cheek humor and brutal violence as Geena Davis' amnesiac wife and mother rediscovers her earlier identity as a ruthless assassin. The pared down *Speed* (1994) set aside such sparring in favor of sequential action set pieces – such as the speeding bus improbably leaping an incomplete section of road – but nonetheless established Sandra Bullock as a star (she continued to have hits in comedy action films such as *Miss Congeniality* [2000] and *The Heat* [2013]) and reinforced Keanu Reeves' ongoing 1990s reinvention as an action performer.

Through the 1990s, action blockbusters such as *Independence Day*, *The Rock* (1996) and *Armageddon* (1998) fine-tuned the aesthetic of motion and machines at work in *Speed*. Filmmaker Michael Bay, whose background was in commercials and music video, became synonymous with a rapid editing style – while criticisms of action as a genre engaged in style over substance were fairly commonplace, this was hardly new. Indeed in his evocation of the commercial logic behind the "Big Loud Action Movie" Larry Gross insists on the longevity of action and spectacle, evoking Fairbanks, Pearl White and David Lean. What has been lost in cinema of the 1990s he implies is thematic complexity (a loss he dates back to the 1970s and the advent of films such as *Star Wars* and *Raiders*); for Gross it is the "psychological complexity, and the registration of accurate social and historical detail," qualities that for him anchored Lean's action epics, such as *Bridge on the River Kwai* (1957) and *Lawrence of Arabia* (1962), that has been lost (2000: 4). Such complexity is replaced by arch references and in-jokes – of the sort later foregrounded in films such as *Charlie's Angels* (2000) or *Pirates of the Caribbean* (2003), movies that require audiences not to take them too seriously. It is as if filmmakers, aware of action cinema's reputation for ideological simplicity and spectacular violence, seek to acknowledge and to revel in the genre's fantastical premises. If this suggests an evolutionary model of action that proceeds from the classical through to self-reflexive action, a historical perspective on action and adventure that view. Films as diverse as the Bourne franchise, *The Lord of the Rings* and *The Hurt Locker* point to the continuation of diverse action and fantasy adventure traditions that are defined by neither action–comedy nor self-reflexive modes.

CHAPTER 3

CRITICAL PERSPECTIVES ON ACTION AND ADVENTURE

Since the 1990s, action and adventure has been a significant genre in film studies scholarship. In the previous chapter, I argued that this stems, at least in part, from action's availability for discussion in terms of generic hybridity. It is also certainly a result of the genre's emergence as a more or less coherent entity and the commercial centrality of action and adventure titles. While there has been some attention within such scholarship to formal questions, critics have most often been concerned with the political significance of action cinema. It is, above all, ideological concerns that have tended to preoccupy critics.

Action has long been regarded as quintessentially popular cinema, generic in the least acceptable sense (simplistic, conservative) and thus outside the aesthetic discourses of value that have developed around Hollywood cinema. On those occasions when an individual film

The Hollywood Action and Adventure Film, First Edition. Yvonne Tasker.
© 2015 John Wiley & Sons, Inc. Published 2015 by John Wiley & Sons, Inc.

with strong action and adventure elements has been well-received, praised for its complexity or formal innovation, that film will typically not be framed as action (or only insofar as it surpasses the superficiality of action). And since, as we've seen, action films typically participate in a range of genres this is easily achieved. *The Terminator* (1984) provides a good example of this process – widely regarded as an entertaining and accomplished genre film, it was initially framed critically as tech-*noir*, or as dystopian science-fiction rather than as action. What is felt to be compelling about the film is its take on future world scenarios, its use of *noir* imagery and time travel themes, rather than say the extended chase sequence format that frames the delivery of these themes. This isn't to say that critics are wrong and that *The Terminator* should be understood primarily as an action film (rather than science-fiction, for example). Rather it is to underline that it is *also* an action film featuring a career-making performance for one of the genre's defining stars of the 1980s and 1990s, Arnold Schwarzenegger, and one that firmly shifted action in a particular direction. Moreover, at a formal level the relentless character of the terminator is expressed not only via the progressive – and visually spectacular – revelation of a machine body beneath the flesh, but through the extended chase sequence format that structures the film. The climactic pursuit sequence enacts the film's themes: future technology has produced a monstrous foe in the terminator, and contemporary machinery ultimately defeats it as Sarah Connor (Linda Hamilton) uses a production line press to crush what remains of the machine/monster.

For mainstream reviewers – and for many scholars – action and adventure are spaces of generic repetition rather than innovation. However, as already noted, action has frequently been at the forefront of the development and refinement of new techniques for conveying visual spectacle. Accordingly, in this chapter I look first at aesthetic perspectives on the action and adventure cinema before turning to what I have termed here *cultural politics*, largely consisting of attempts by critics to pin down the meaning and ideological significance of action and adventure, genres that are widely regarded as conservative modes of filmmaking that deploy and endorse conventional stereotypes of nation, gender, race and class.

Action Aesthetics: Exhilaration and Destruction

One of the most persistent debates about action aesthetics has been to do with spectacle. Consider the titles of books such as King's *Spectacular Narratives*, Arroyo's *Action / Spectacle Cinema*, Lichtenfeld's *Action Speaks Louder: Violence, Spectacle and the American Action Movie* and my own *Spectacular Bodies*. These studies share an interest in the aesthetics as much as the ideological work of action cinema. All argue that spectacle and narrative cannot be simply separated. Despite routine assumptions to the contrary, King writes: "Narrative is far from being eclipsed, even in the most spectacular and effects-oriented of today's blockbuster attractions" (2000: 2).

One of the marked features of writings on action cinema since the 2000s is a desire to explore the distinctive features of action aesthetics. Setting aside assumptions about the genres simplicity, critics have begun to unpack what King terms the "explosive rhetorics of the contemporary action cinema" (2000: 3). One strategy is to think about the genre's formal and thematic operations via analogies with other genres that have been explored more extensively. The Western is perhaps the most common reference point along with the musical, the war film an being obvious yet less developed genre connection.

PLATE 3.1 *Mission: Impossible:* with an emphasis on composition, movement and sound, the action set-piece has often been compared to the musical number (1996, directed by Brian De Palma and produced by Paramount Pictures and Cruise/Wagner Productions).

Arroyo is among the critics to pursue a structural analogy between the action set-piece and the musical number. He reads *Mission: Impossible* – "gleefully superficial" – as a film constructed around its set-pieces, "each involving some element of action and ingenuity … woven through the film like songs and dances in an old-fashioned musical" (2000: 23). Almost 30 years earlier Ian Cameron drew a similar analogy, writing that "The transference of this sort of swash-buckling tale [he refers specifically to the novels of Alexandre Dumas] to the cinema produces movies that have much in common with musicals, with action sequences such as swordfights taking the place of dance numbers" (1973: 89). The connections between action and melodrama emphasized by silent film historian Ben Singer, equally underline the expression of emotional intensity through formal elements rather than dialogue.

King too picks up on the musical as a reference point for the action film. He offers a detailed analysis of action sequences (numbers) from Spielberg's *Jurassic Park* (1993), showing how the thematic concerns of the narrative are developed in these sequences and rejecting the commonly expressed view with that the genre – and spectacular cinema more generally – signals the demise of narrative. Of course since *Jurassic Park* was widely regarded as setting new standards with regard to digital effects work – the interaction of human actors and digital dinosaurs – it is unsurprising that such spectacular aspects of the film were kept to the fore. Yet King's analysis works to underline the *meaningful* character of the spectacle in Spielberg's movie. And while this book explores a more extended generic history than that linked to contemporary action/spectacle, King's articulation of what he terms "thematic narrative structures" (2000: 2) is nonetheless highly productive for a consideration of action and adventure more broadly. Indeed his insistence that narrative and spectacle work together in diverse and at times quite complex ways is echoed and developed by theorist Lisa Purse who argues that this connection is fundamental for an understanding of action and adventure as a genre.

Purse interrogates precisely what is at stake in the term "spectacle," so often applied to the genre. She notes that spectacle can relate either to the presentation of "something beyond the realm of everyday experience" or to "the mode of presentation" (2011: 28). Here, she identifies a second formal feature of action cinema; the use of an array of techniques to enhance the visual spectacle. Thus qualities of pace, achieved through the manipulation of sound or editing, are as significant formally as *mise-en-scéne*. Drawing attention to the structure of action set-pieces via a comparison with the musical's dance numbers involves not only an implication that action advances the narrative, but also the framing of violence as choreography (historically of course action sequences pre-dated the musical; nevertheless both are painstakingly choreographed). Indeed the analogy with the musical works in part since it requires us to set aside the violence and destruction that forms much of the spectacular content within action cinema, to appreciate the formal elements of the images and sequences thus organized. It additionally works to foreground (1) sound and (2) the importance of movement, whether of the camera and of characters/objects within the frame.

Movement of the elements within the frame and the impression of movement achieved via cutting operate as crucial aspects of the orchestrated design of an action aesthetic. Though conventions have changed over time, the centrality of movement has remained. From single-camera chase sequences through the deployment of cross-cutting as a vehicle for suspense to the increasingly elaborate editing of action in the 1990s (of which more later) and the development of ever-more compelling digital effects in the twenty-first century, action, critics agree, is a sensational, even a sensual cinema. Ian Cameron writes that "adventure movies can … work very powerfully on a sensual level of sheer physical exhilaration" (1973: 57). When filmmaker Kathryn Bigelow speaks in this same vein – remarking that "action movies have a capacity to be pure cinema" (1991: 313) – she recalls longstanding debates in film theory as to the essence of cinema as a medium.

Tom Gunning's influential work on early cinema posits a 'cinema of attractions;' refusing the clarity of a distinction between Lumière's actuality films and Méliès' fantasies, Gunning points to the early cinema's "harnessing of visibility" for pleasure. He cites cubist artist Fernand Léger's observation that the new medium's power and potential was "a matter of *making images seen*," and invokes the futurist Marinetti's praise for variety theatre as a form that encouraged active spectators as well as deploying "aesthetics of astonishment and stimulation" (1986: 56, 59). This element of cinema as a form crafted for spectacle, that tendency operating subsequently in productive tension with narrative, has a particular resonance for action cinema. Indeed Gunning's passing comment on the contemporary manifestation/continuation of the tendencies he explores in early cinema makes this explicit: "in some sense recent spectacle cinema has reaffirmed its roots in stimulus and carnival rides, in what might be called the Spielberg–Lucas–Coppola cinema of effects" (1986: 61). Gunning expresses no particular enthusiasm for these developments ("effects are tamed attractions," he writes). Nonetheless his observations prove fruitful for a consideration of action as a spectacular cinema since they underline the importance of sensation. The significance of spectacle – and its intimate relationship to narrative – recurs throughout this book. Above all, action and adventure cinema reminds us (audiences and critics alike) of film as an emphatically visual medium, a form in which something is there to be *seen*.

While both spectacular sets and location shooting construct an exhilarating impression of space in adventure films as diverse as *National Treasure* (2007), *King Solomon's Mines* (1950) or *Lawrence of Arabia* (1962), editing has long been used to generated suspense and excitement within action genres. Increasingly rapid editing was a characteristic of action in the 1990s, facilitated as Lichtenfeld notes via developments in digital editing and playback, techniques that he sees as making possible what he regards as "over-cutting" in films such as *The Rock*. In the previous decade however a similar set of concerns had been encapsulated in the phrase "MTV aesthetics" with the stylish and heavily action-oriented crime show *Miami Vice* (NBC, 1984–1989) exemplifying the application of music video techniques to narrative-based television genres. Bordwell couples decreasing shot length to three other techniques in contemporary film style: tight framing in dialogue scenes, bipolar extremes of lens length and greater use of camera movement. Together this intensified continuity produces "an aesthetic of broad but forceful effects" (2002: 24) that impacts on filmmakers, performers (requiring different acting techniques) and audiences since, "as styles change, so do viewing skills" (2002: 25).

The evocation of Tom Gunning's work underlines how writing on action aesthetics has drawn on early and silent cinema scholarship. As discussed in Chapter 2, action featured in the earliest developments of cinema with an interest in the possibilities of movement within the frame (the train arriving at the station) and the use of journeys (fantastical or otherwise) and chases as narrative frames. The longevity of these conventions is in itself noteworthy. Some have explored further the dynamism of early action and the distinctiveness of an action aesthetic. Ben Singer's *Melodrama and Modernity* offers a compelling account of early cinema that underlines the connections between melodrama and action: thrills and spectacle, virtue in peril. For both Singer and Jennifer Bean, modernity provides a crucial context for the development of early action/melodrama, its heroes and heroines negotiating a rapidly transforming world.

In a more recent historical moment, questions of action aesthetics have been caught up the developing impact of digital technologies. The significance of these technologies for editing has already been mentioned. Digitally created or enhanced action spectacle has become an increasing presence within the genre, in particular within the blockbuster in which it allows the imagining of impossible feats in newly plausible ways. The particular re-emergence of the superhero film, the focus of this book's final chapter, Chapter 11, is clearly linked to the development of digital imaging with the use of computers alongside conventional studio and location work central to the effects of a film such as *Iron Man* (2008). Given the emphasis on authenticity in much action cinema discourse, computer generated imagery has proven fascinating and at times problematic. Indeed the insistence on the part of performers on the training undertaken for their action roles suggests an investment in action authenticity of a quite particular kind.

Adventure Cinema: Narrative, Space and Time

Adventure cinema – along with the action sequences it typically and spectacularly stages – is a vital yet relatively unexplored component of Hollywood filmmaking. From its early days, Hollywood has crafted movies from adventure stories. Some were original but many were adapted from popular sources (books for example, such as *King Solomon's Mines* [1885], *She* [1887] or *Treasure Island* [1883]) or from characters featured in popular media from folk tales (the numerous versions of *Robin Hood*) and magazines (or later comic books).

Adventure films locate their characters in settings that not only permit but seem to require heroic action. Whether everyday figures who inadvertently embark on adventure, or heroic figures who actively seek it out, adventure films show men and women calling on reserves of courage, wit and physical ability. Action is always involved with scenes of pursuit, combat and spectacle moving the narrative onwards.

Adventure cinema frequently presents the personal development of the major characters – their growth or maturation – in parallel with the journey they embark on, or the task they must undertake. Facing the challenges of adventure becomes an exercise in character building then, although the genre is not associated with particularly complex characterization or motivation. In different film versions of the tale, Robin Hood is seen to grow up and accept responsibility through the course of his conflict with the Sherriff of Nottingham and other villains, and through his developing love for Maid Marion. Sometimes adventure narratives center on female characters, as with pirate adventure *Anne of the Indies* (1951) in which Jean Peters plays Captain Anne Providence. Here romance may play a larger part, but the basic structure is unchanged: adventure allows growth and personal development, albeit of a limited kind, amidst the battles and spectacle – in *Anne of the Indies*, Providence will ultimately forego her plans of vengeance and sacrifice herself for her beloved LaRochelle (Louis Jourdan). *Pirates of the Caribbean* serves as a later example in which the female lead is an active participant in the adventure. More often, however, female characters in adventure narratives tend to be passive figures, awaiting rescue.

The cinematic construction of adventure space operates in geographic and temporal terms. Frequently adventure narratives involve a journey into uncharted, unfamiliar or dangerous terrain: exotic locales of one kind or another are a staple of the genre. The journey undertaken by Jane Parker (Maureen O'Sullivan) and her father in *Tarzan the Ape Man* (1932), for example, takes them into spaces referred to on the map only as "unknown territory." In *She* (1935), the party trek through the Artic to a lost icy land. Fantasy adventure movies *The 7th Voyage of Sinbad* (1958) or *Jason and the Argonauts* (1963) involve dangerous journeys and battle with mythical creatures including Cyclops, a hydra and skeleton warriors. New Hollywood films that allude to or rework Hollywood's adventure tradition – notably the Indiana Jones films directed by Steven Spielberg – also prominently feature lengthy journeys signaled through the imagery of an advancing line on a map. So these adventure films build on – and give spectacular visual form to – popular fictions that celebrated fantastic voyages or quests of one kind or another. French writer Jules Verne's books took his characters under the sea, around the world, to orbit the Moon and to the center of the Earth. One of the earliest fantasy films routinely cited in histories of cinema is Georges Méliès *Le Voyage dans la Lune/A Trip to the Moon* (1902) a film that acknowledges Verne (whose novels were published as *Voyages Extraordinaries*).

What we can call adventure space in the cinema – spaces that may or may not exist in actuality but perform a function in the story-world of facilitating adventure – isn't always a matter of fantastic panoramas or journeys into lost worlds. Hollywood films also exploit more intimate and even claustrophobic spaces via the discovery of secret passageways, lost caves, hidden treasures and so on. Disney's *National Treasure* (2004, 2007) movies revel in such devices; part travelogue with detours in various US and UK cities, the films turn famous American heritage sites into places of fantastical adventure.

The second dimension of cinematic adventure is the temporal. On occasion adventure movies employ time travel devices, but more often adventure cinemas simply use past or future settings to provide a suitably removed environment for heroic action. Adventure cinema frequently evokes an historical past, whether actual, folkloric, mythical or some combination of these. Typical adventure settings include: Merrie England, the Ancient world, imperial adventure, the heyday of piracy in the 1700s, and the musketeers of Dumas' seventeenth-century France. Removing the action to an earlier time allows a similar displacement to the geographical remove achieved in films like *Jurassic Park* with its unspecified Pacific island; the effect is to enact a scenario that is in some senses familiar but which takes place in a fantastical setting. The title cards of the 1922 *Robin Hood*, starring Douglas Fairbanks, frame the film as a "compound of legend and chronicle," acknowledging the fantastical rendition of period detail that is central to adventure cinema's pleasures; thus a montage of ruined buildings gives way to Hollywood's recreation of a functioning castle, suggesting both historical authenticity and movie world fantasy.

Cameron remarks that "the one unlikely location for adventure is here and now, a perspective that underlines the fantastical character of the genre" (1973: 71). Taves is more concerned with temporal than geographic displacement (although the latter does feature in his discussion of imperial adventure). Discussing what he terms historical adventure, which he divides into five main types, Taves argues that "Adventure in the cinema deals primarily with liberty and over-coming oppression as a historical phenomenon" (1993: 13). While this framework allows a fascinating excavation of these types, the wider traditions of adventure cinema are effectively (indeed explicitly) excluded from his account. And of course the dimensions of time and space can be, and often are, connected in cinema's adventure space ("A long time ago in a galaxy, far, far away ..." as the opening scrolling text of *Star Wars* has it). *The Lost World* follows its groups of explorers onto a "plateau that time forgot"; there they encounter dinosaurs, fabu-lously recreated via stop motion. The explorers bring a brontosaurus back to London where its escape causes havoc in a precursor of the narrative of *King Kong* in which the clash of nature and culture ends with the dramatic destruction of Kong.

In his analysis of the action films *Die Hard* and *Speed*, Martin Flannagan uses Bakhtin's work on the adventure story to theorize the particular articulation of time and space in action cinema, a form invested in an impression of movement through space. Adventure time is not like time as we experience it in life, marked by change and aging: "Series such as the Bond films or *Die Hard* can endlessly prop-agate themselves because their form, the very time and space of which they are constituted and within which their adventures unfold, is so adaptable, elastic, abstract" (2004: 116).

Whether they involve geographical or temporal shifts, or both, the journeys undertaken require the characters of adventure narratives to demonstrate qualities such as bravery, resilience, strength and resource-fulness. Themes of maturation and personal development (albeit rather conventional) are pronounced, with characters frequently presented as either growing up or learning about their abilities and desires through their adventures. Often this process is staged around the male hero, as in *The Thief of Bagdad* discussed in Chapter 4. Where this growth pro-cess takes place around female characters, it is typically figured in rather different terms.

As Cynthia Erb notes, the MGM Tarzan films that exemplify the popular jungle adventure trend of the 1930s, center as much on Jane

Parker as on Tarzan himself. On her arrival in Africa, Jane declares herself to have set aside civilization – associated in the adventure tradition with social rules and conventional gender roles – embracing what she terms a "savage" sense of self. Jane insists on accompanying her father on his quest for an elephant's graveyard and the riches in ivory it can yield. *En route* she encounters Tarzan, played here by champion swimmer and Hollywood pin-up Johnny Weissmuller. Jane's interest in Tarzan links adventure with both romance and sexual opportunity. Although the multiple Tarzan films were limited by censorship – with Jane's costume in the 1934 *Tarzan and His Mate* a particular point of contention – they nonetheless underline that both female and male characters participated in the adventures Hollywood staged in exotic locations. In such ways the adventure tradition exploited such spatial relocations to challenge the gendered norms of the time whether in costume or behavior. In *The Lost World*, Paula (Bessie Love) finds love in a space marked as free from conventions and social obligations – although we are swiftly informed that one of professors in the party used to be a minister and will thus be able to marry the happy couple.

PLATE 3.2 Adventure space offers female characters opportunities for freedom from social constraints. Jane Parker (Maureen O'Sullivan) and Tarzan (Johnny Weissmuller) in *Tarzan the Ape Man* (1932, directed by W.S. Van Dyke and produced by Metro-Goldwyn-Mayer (MGM)).

Films such as *The Lost World* and *Tarzan the Ape Man* also fore-ground the extent to which evolutionary ideas of the primitive – in contrast to the supposedly civilized explorers – are central to the adventure tradition. Within Hollywood's repertoire of action genres more broadly the Western has been a key locus for an exploration of these themes with settlers, cowboys and gunmen pitted against native peoples and hostile natural environments. As the example of the Western illustrates, action and adventure cinema frequently mobilize racial discourses of superiority and subordination. Both the geographical and temporal settings of adventure cinema involve imperial history and associated hierarchies of race. The genre pres-ents – and occasionally confronts – racial stereotypes, from clichés of Latin passion to Orientalist fantasies of feminized Asia or con-structions of native peoples as primitive or childlike. From Westerns to jungle adventure, adventurers move through landscapes that free them from the bounds of convention, involving assumptions about simple or natural modes of living. Adventure films thus routinely oppose the confined lives and artifice of the ruling group to the freedom (even, ironically, freedom in oppression) of the people; the romanticizing of rebellious pirates, outlaw heroes and their uncon-ventional modes of living functions as a commentary on the values of the day.

Conflict and quest are key narrative principles of adventure and action – conflict typically drives the action. In terms of critical per-spectives on action and adventure, the place and meaning of violence is central. All action and adventure films feature violence to varying degrees. Yet violence is no straightforward cinematic sign; its meaning is determined by context. Violence is handled in a quite particular manner within adventure cinema. Taves writes: "Much of adventure's commitment to a largely fictionalized historical past is evident in the genre's treatment of violence, which is far different from most other action forms". He regards the violence of adventure cinema as inno-cent: "Although revolutions and battles proliferate in adventure, fighting is usually slick and almost bloodless, presented in an innocent and often playful manner."(1993: 104). This is certainly true of the fights in *The Adventures of Robin Hood*; nonetheless the fights in adven-ture cinema express the underlying themes and while they may be bloodless, they are nonetheless intense.

While it seems obvious that the resonance of violence in war movies is different from that of historical adventure (a difference that has to do with the status of represented events), critics are less clear on the ways in which the earnest yet cheerful swordfights of historical adventure might be distinguished from the lacerated bodies and exploding buildings of 1980s action, for instance. Writing on the Western, Ed Buscombe comments on violence and action:

> At the centre of the Western as it evolved in the cinema, and at the centre of the popular fiction which was its immediate predecessor, was physical action: the violent confrontation between men and nature, or even more crucially, between savage or outlaw and the representative of advance civilizations. (1988: 18)

For Buscombe then, action is closely connected to the meaning and thematic concerns of the Western genre. The observation applies to action cinema more generally: thus in the exploration of the violent imagery of conflict, questions of aesthetics increasingly shift onto and overlap with questions of meaning.

The Cultural Politics of Action

When we understand genre as having a ritual function, myths of redemptive or regenerative violence become fascinating sites of cultural work. It is within debates regarding cultural politics that action and adventure cinema has been most critically contested. Here, violence has been insistently coupled to ideological questions of might and state power, whether via the association of Rambo and Reagan, the vigilantism of Harry Callahan and so on. Despite its generic diversity, all action and adventure films center on some form of conflict: as such there are shared themes and recurrent critical preoccupations to do with the ideological work of these films. At its simplest level, we can ask, who wields power and over whom in the action cinema world? Perspectives on the Western or debates around the apparent endorsement of rogue cop justice in films such as *Dirty Harry* generate a context in which action – and particularly violent action – is frequently read politically as a conservative articulation of white masculine strength.

Scholarship on action and adventure narratives has been particularly interested in exploring meaning and ideology, foregrounding the presentation of nation, empire, gender, race and social order. Given the genre's tendency to rely on broad-brush characterization, a consideration of stereotypes is unsurprisingly common as an approach. What does the hero look like – is he always a white man, for instance? Who are the villains or opponents and how are they characterized? In the years since the terrorist attacks on New York in September 2001, an interest has developed in the portrayal of the war on terror and of Arab and other groups. Given that action films typically present violence as redemptive, forging and protecting society even at times at the cost of the hero, it is unsurprising that these political questions remain high on the critical agenda. In this context, both King and Lichtenfeld foreground an interest in frontier myths. Appealing to national origin stories, the frontier articulates America as a developing, provisional space in which the hero's violence is required to preserve the law.

Susan Jeffords' influential formulation of hard-bodied action heroism suggested a series of analogies between the films and politics of the Reagan era. She writes of a broad set of "correspondences between the public and popular images of 'Ronald Reagan' and the action-adventure films that portrayed many of the same narratives of heroism, success, achievement, toughness, strength, and 'good old Americanness' that made the Reagan Revolution possible" (1993: 15). Jeffords' account effectively couples attention to Reagan's desire to shrink government and the anti-government/officialdom rhetoric of films such as *Rambo: First Blood Part II*. Moreover, she underlines the importance of the body in both cinematic and political imagery, formulating the evocative figure of the era's preferred "hard body," opposed to the "errant" soft bodies of liberals and the peoples they stood for. Jeffords writes that the "depiction of the indefatigable, muscular, and invincible masculine body became the emblem not only for the Reagan presidency but for its ideologies and economies as well" (1993: 25). The extension of this analysis into cinema takes Jeffords to Rambo, "one of the most popular icons of the Reagan era" (1993: 28).

However, the critical focus on action film and politics or ideology is not straightforward. The condemnation of *Dirty Harry* as a fascist film by Pauline Kael (1972) – she was by no means alone in adopting this stance (Roger Ebert [1972] shared her view) – represents a genuine expression of disgust and exasperation on the part of a high profile critic. Using films or indeed any form of culture, as a reference point to explore contemporary concerns offers a strategy for the critic or essayist and it is common in such forms to employ hyperbole. But what does it mean to make such connections within a scholarly context?

The relationship between culture and politics is complex, but certainly relevant for a consideration of action cinema, a genre that has frequently been characterized as conservative. Jeffords is careful to explain that she is not crediting the films she discusses with a conscious political agenda. Rather, her view is that they participate in the same cultural moment and that discussion of cinematic and political discourses allows a fuller understanding of their interaction. In the process Jeffords generates a metaphor of the hard body that allows her to think through the visual rhetoric of the period. Jeffords' analysis situates the muscular action stars of the 1980s against the conservative context of New Right ideologies and economics, suggesting the formation of a rhetorical association between the white, male hard body and the nation itself.

Although certainly a central component in the genre's success, the aesthetics of action are not particularly relevant to this discursive approach. Without suggesting that these questions of an uncanny correspondence – at times compelling – between cinema and Reaganite rhetoric should be set aside, it is important to understand what is overlooked in the emphasis on cultural politics that long characterized discussion of action. Taking the lengthy movie career of the Rambo character played by Stallone as a reference point, Carl Boggs and Tom Pollard pursue a political critique of Hollywood cinema and wider American culture. Thus they insist on a "linkage between the actuality of war, militarism, and violence in a media culture that celebrates that actuality" (2008: 578). Action has a privileged place in this critique as a genre that exemplifies "a growing media and popular indulgence of the militarization of American society" (2008: 573). Such perspectives require engagement, but also caution. Frequently they involve not only a gloss on the behavior and attitudes of high profile politicians, but a simplistic characterization of the audience. Across journalistic and scholarly writing, the action movie is found wanting and audiences described as troubling for their participatory pleasure in violence.

Scholars have often found the particular resonance of action in its foregrounding of cultural concerns – as, for example, in my own work, or that of Jeffords on questions of gender and politics, drawing attention to the action cinema's importance as a space for the elaboration of new formations of masculinity. My work on these questions of American masculinity via the action film sought to foreground the new prominence of the muscular male body within Hollywood cinema. *Spectacular Bodies* emphasizes the eroticized display of built male bodies as not only a sign of masculine strength (though they may also be characterized in this way) but functioning thematically as a site of power and powerlessness – the hero's physically powerful body set in a scenario of struggle against obstacles physical and social. Lisa Purse develops these themes in her analysis of twenty-first century action, arguing that at both formal and narrative levels the genre is concerned with more generalized themes of mastery.

While Jeffords sees the hard body as implicitly endorsing the militarism of the 1980s, the decade's action cinema also foregrounds questions of class, albeit in the populist terms of American culture that emphasizes resistance to authority rather than the organization of labor associated with activist cinema around class. In contrast to both these perspectives, historical studies seek by contrast to explore the texture of culture, the way in which wartime films, for example, might be experienced by the audiences who were exposed to them. The display of the male body in Hollywood cinema was not a phenomenon exclusive to the 1980s; beefcake imagery was associated with athletic stars such as Johnny Weissmuller in the 1930s and 1940s, Burt Lancaster in the 1950s or Rock Hudson in the 1960s. With respect to cultural interpretation of the male star image, Gaylyn Studlar situates Fairbanks' athletic star persona in the context of 1920s discourses of masculinity in crisis, underlining how his persona appealed to a boyish discourse of the rewards of energy and exercise.

Race and Action–Adventure Cinema

With their free use of foreign and unfamiliar spaces (as well as those that are outright imaginary) as settings for heroic exploits, adventure movies suggest that the world is uniquely available to the hero. Writing of adventure and colonialism, Taves notes both that "empire is a place of opportunity" in the genre, and that films in this tradition encompass both a documentary impulse – detailing for cinema audiences the customs, costumes and language of unfamiliar parts of the world – and a more generalized space for adventure. Colonial settings, he writes, serve "primarily as a site for courageous deeds against a background often more mythic than factual in its historical details" (1993: 174). Unsurprisingly then, hierarchies of race and nationality are strongly in evidence in such film traditions.

Colonial adventures typically articulate racial and national hierarchies in which (mostly white) European and American explorers encounter African, Asian and other peoples characterized as racially other. Black Africans are typically primitive in the Tarzan films; at times menacing but more often simply part of the background – native people provide a form of "local color." It is tempting to consider the sorts of stereotypes seen in *Tarzan of the Apes*, in which the pygmy tribe attempt to sacrifice the explorers to a giant gorilla (an oddly artificial threat when set against the extensive use of actual animal footage in the movie), as a relic of the past, belonging to a period of filmmaking in which the prejudices of the wider culture were routinely reinforced. Yet more recent adventure films such as *Indiana Jones and the Temple of Doom* (1984) and *Pirates of the Caribbean: Dead Man's Chest* (2006) deploy racial stereotypes as part of their recycling of earlier film traditions: the murderous Thugees of *Temple of Doom*, central to the film's plot, caused offense and aroused controversy, while the comedy cannibals of *Dead Man's Chest*, minor characters in the film's narrative, or the equation of Tia Dalma (Naomie Harris) with magic and with destructive forces of nature – the "dreadlocked soothsayer mistress" (2008: 135) of the swamps as Stephane Dunn puts it – went largely unremarked upon. As we'll see, more subtle forms of racial hierarchy continue to feature in both action and adventure cinema. As such, studying these traditions involves thinking closely about issues of race and representation.

The analysis of race and racism through action has been an important feature of scholarship around the genre. In part this is a function of the genre's use of relatively crude racial stereotypes, in part a consequence of an emphasis on physicality and the body. Equally though, the fact that action and adventure are forms that have given greater opportunities to African-American stars than any other genre bar comedy is a significant factor. As discussed in the historical overview in Chapter 2, major African-American stars such as Will Smith and Denzel Washington have been strongly associated with action roles. And yet these films rarely acknowledge race or racial hierarchies, other than as something that can be simply moved past. The advent of the bi-racial buddy formula in the 1980s – with films such as *48 Hrs.* (1982) and *Lethal Weapon* (1987) – also led to critical interest in the commercial origins and ideological significance of this pairing, with Guerrero (1993) reading it as a strategy for containment. That is, black actors and characters achieve more prominence but only in certain roles, typically subordinate.

In this context, black action films of the 1970s sought not only to position African-Americans in leading roles but to challenge the stereotypes so routinely deployed in Hollywood cinema. As Dunn writes, "The fantasy that these films marketed to black moviegoers was the spectacular reversal of the racial and/or patriarchal status quo, tapping into the social reality of racial oppression and racial tensions" (2008: 5). The powerful male protagonists of the independently produced *Sweet Sweetback's Badasssss Song* (1971) and *Shaft* (produced the same year for MGM) negotiate the city with intelligence and violence. Their mastery is associated with sexuality in a symbolic world that leaves little space for more challenging portrayals of African-American women. Nonetheless while black action cinema is often characterized as exploiting masculinist discourse, the visibility of the violent black female protagonist of action is also an important part of the moment. Pam Grier, star of *Coffy* (1973) and *Foxy Brown* (1974), is undoubtedly the best known. Other Blaxploitation action films with female leads or prominent female action figures were produced within Hollywood such as *Cleopatra Jones* (1973) or *Black Belt Jones* (1974, featuring Gloria Hendry who had appeared as a romantic figure for Bond in the previous year's *Live and Let Die*; here she supports Jim Kelly, seen alongside Bruce Lee in *Enter the Dragon*, also 1973). An emphasis on the body whether sexual or glamorous means that these films present their action women as emphatically female in contrast to the more androgynous white action women of the 1980s (Ripley in *Aliens* for example). Precursors of the sexualized action women of the 1990s, black action films showcase a fantasy of specifically female mastery.

While action moved to occupy a position of prominence in terms of commercial success, black women in action have not retained the visibility of the 1970s films. One exception was *Fatal Beauty* (1987), a film that followed *Beverley Hills Cop* in casting a successful African-American comedian, Whoopi Goldberg, as an unconventional cop in the privileged/surreal context of California. Promotional images featured Goldberg as Detective Rita Rizzoli reclining in a pink Cadillac; wearing sneakers (her feet rest on the car door) she holds her gun casually, seemingly more as a prop than as a cop poised for action. The Hollywood sign in the background signals the affluent location against which the film's scenario of crime and drugs will take place. In contrast to the 1970s Blaxploitation representation of black women in action – images that coupled sex and violence – Goldberg's Rizzoli is desexualized, her relationship with co-star Sam Elliott cut back, reinforcing the character's isolation in a hostile world.

The women drawn into and enacting violence in *Set it Off* (1996) explicitly respond to the class and racial hierarchies of American society, deploying urban action and crime conventions

PLATE 3.3 While black action has been highly visible within Hollywood, racial hierarchies and stereotypes are rarely interrogated. Halle Berry's role as the iconic Storm in the *X-Men* (here in *X-Men: The Last Stand*) films suggests some of the possibilities and the limits of Hollywood action (2006, directed by Brett Ratner and produced by Twentieth Century Fox Film Corporation, Marvel Enterprises, Donners' Company, Ingenious Film Partners, Dune Entertainment, Major Studio Partners, Bad Hat Harry Productions, X3 Canada Productions, X3US Productions, XM3 Service and thinkfilm).

to portray women with limited choices. More in line with Hollywood's trend towards "beauty in motion" was Halle Berry's much derided turn as *Catwoman*, a film that evokes some sort of mystical lineage to ancient Egypt. Berry's action roles as Storm in *X-Men* (2000) and as CIA agent Jinx Johnson in Bond film *Die Another Day* (2002) underline her success in ensemble pieces and supporting roles. As Dunn writes of the genre more broadly, "as surreal and spectacular as the arena of action cinema remains, it is like popular movies by and large, a landscape that has trouble envisioning black femaleness" (2008: 135).

Women in Action: Theoretical Perspectives on Gender and Agency

Much film studies scholarship is underwritten by an assumption that genres can be understood as gendered. That is some genres are regarded as male or masculine, others as female or feminine. The common use of terms such as "chick flick" in reviewing practices reinforces such designations. These assumptions are very much in evidence in writings on action and adventure cinema. Rick Altman, for example, in discussing promotional strategies from the classical era suggests that adventure is broadly for men in the audience and romance is correspondingly for women (2000: 57). For Peter Krämer the immense commercial success of James Cameron's 1997 blockbuster *Titanic* lay in its ability to combine the concerns of a male audience, which he deems to be an interest in action and adventure and those of a female audience, which for him means romance. The film, he argues was not only "marketed as an epic love story" but was "concerned with the complex narrative exploration of female subjectivity, of romantic and other feelings" (1998: 613). While Krämer is almost certainly right that these assumptions about audience interest are prevalent in a film industry that, though broadly liberal, tends to conservatism with respect to gender, the very success of *Titanic* underlines the need to look past these gendered assumptions. With its strong female protagonist and proto-feminist narrative of resistance against early twentieth-century social norms, *Titanic* exemplifies a lively Hollywood tradition of including women in the action as well as the romance. Dunn, too, in her account of Blaxploitation notes the critical tendency to down-play the interests of female audiences, suggesting that despite the prob-lematic stereotypes at work, "black women may negotiate the racial and gender politics underlying the narrative" finding "various types of pleasure in viewing action cinema generally and the rare fantasies of a baad black woman heroine, especially one headlining a Hollywood film" (2008: 16).

One reason why such strong female characters may be overlooked in the context of action has to do with their relative importance within the story world. Rose's prominence in *Titanic* is not neces-sarily typical. Women often feature in action and adventure as sup-porting characters, frequently offering the possibility of a romantic connection for the male hero who has previously lived either an isolated life or within a group of men. Angela Bassett's Mace in *Strange Days* is a case in point, a charismatic figure who moves from the margins of the narrative to occupy a more central position in the film's concerns although the obsessions of friend Lenny (Ralph Fiennes) remain at the center of the film that ends with the two in a brief almost dreamlike embrace. Many silent and classical adventure films end with the formation of a romantic couple as do both *The Thief of Bagdad* and *The Adventures of Robin Hood*, discussed in Chapter 4.

While female characters may occupy a role that positions them as romantic or sexual object of interest for the hero and, as a consequence, a figure in peril, they do feature as combative or active figures within the genre. In horror, science-fiction and fantasy formats, female action heroes are more in evidence: as an adventurer in *Lara Croft: Tomb Raider* (2001) or battling zombie hordes in *Resident Evil* (2002). In movies framed around military or militarized teams, women feature in ways that are at times unremarked, as for example with Michelle Rodriguez's role in *Battle: Los Angeles* (2011). Indeed, as we've seen in the previous chapters, the location of women as sidekicks, partners or main protagonist of action has shifted over time and goes back to the early days of Hollywood filmmaking. So too feminist analyses of and engagement with the action genre has developed over time, ranging from disinterest and critique to celebration.

While feminist scholarship has not engaged with films such as *Anne of the Indies* and *Sons of the Musketeers*, cited by Taves as examples of the female hero type, an increasing body of feminist work took as its object the action cinema, particularly as the genre shifted to incorporate higher profile female roles. The 1980s saw action cinema significantly increase its visibility via powerful iconic male images, rapidly expanding budgets and extraordinary box office success. While Hollywood action movies frequently minimized the narrative significance accorded to female characters, notably in the hard-bodied formulations discussed previously, from the second half of the 1980s the action heroine too achieved greater prominence. James Cameron's *Aliens* (1986), a sequel to *Alien* (1979) restyled Sigourney Weaver's Ripley as, in her words, "Rambolina" in a film that juxtaposed science-fiction, action and war movie conventions culminating in a monster movie showdown between Ripley and the mother alien. Weaver's playful self-designation resonates with critical perspectives that suggested that Hollywood's female action heroes were little more than figurative males.

Female action heroes emerge as challenging figures with respect to the genre's usual iconography. If women have often played a supporting role, functioned as a prize or passively awaited rescue, how do we theorize an alternative construction of gender in the genre? Feminist criticism had long scrutinized Hollywood in terms of its tendency to relegate female characters to positions that lacked narrative agency and that foregrounded their function as sexual spectacle (the figure of the showgirl in the Western, for instance). One of the most influential essays in feminist film studies, Laura Mulvey's 1975 "Visual Pleasure and Narrative Cinema," characterizes Hollywood cinema as organized around a "male gaze" for which women serve as an erotic object, defined as feminine figures who wait. Mulvey uses Freudian and Lacanian concepts to theorize this, for her inescapable, visual hierarchy. Certainly the tendency to portray action women in relentlessly sexual terms underlines the relevance of these perspectives. As indeed does the impulse to "explain" female action via backstories that frame their violence in terms of a search for justice or revenge, a maternal impulse or a paternal legacy.

As noted here, black women have not figured prominently as action heroes in Hollywood cinema. Latina action heroines have become more visible in the genre as seen, for example, in Michelle Rodriguez's association with tough, action roles in films including *The Fast and the*

Furious (2001) and *Resident Evil*. Mary Beltrán has persuasively analyzed the ambivalence of this development, writing:

> Latina action protagonists, whether read as Latina and thus of mixed racial heritage or as ethnically ambiguous, arguably provide a visual and ideological reference that is compelling to audiences today. Embodying cultural concerns ... the *más macha* heroine is both an of-the-moment cinematic role model symbolizing Latina and national progress on a number of fronts, and a smokescreen in relation to inequities that continue to prevent many Latinas from gaining power in real life. (2004: 197–198)

Along these lines feminist scholarship has extensively debated the significance of Hollywood's latest generation of action women. To what extent, critics have asked, did tough, even masculine, images of women in action trouble the gender hierarchies of the popular cinema or simply exploit a sexualized image of female violence? The incorporation of romantic interest for female characters was frequently read as containment, a problematic reinscription of femininity. My concept of "musculinity" was developed as a way of reading such images, foregrounding the performative dimensions of gender with respect to these buff female figures: "'Musculinity' indicates the way in which the signifiers of strength are not limited to male characters" (Tasker, 1993: 149). It also underlines that Hollywood's action heroines are still very much marked as women. In this way we acknowledge the particular narrative and visual strategies for signaling female vulnerability as part of "the extreme images of bodily vulnerability and invulnerability that are mobilised in the action cinema" (Tasker, 1993: 150). While feminist scholarship debated the masculinized imagery of the action heroine, the genre developed a rather different presentation of women in action. The tongue in cheek tone of mainstream action lent itself to a quality of parody that was exploited to the full in action films such as *The Long Kiss Goodnight* and *The Quick and the Dead* (1995).

Hollywood has long framed active or powerful women in terms of sexuality. Foregrounding women's sexuality, their function as spectacle, has rather different connotations than the foregrounding of the male body in 1980s and 1990s action cinema: contrast for example, the gradual stages of undress of John McClane in *Die Hard* and that of

Alice (Mila Jovovich) in the *Resident Evil* series. Towards the end of the 1990s Hollywood cinema began to foreground (or return to the fore) an explicitly glamorous, sexualized version of the action heroine in titles such as *Charlie's Angels, Lara Croft: Tomb Raider* (2001) and *X-Men* (2000). Described by Marc O'Day as "action babes" and by Cristina Lucia Stasia as examples of the "postfeminist action film," the toned bodies of these film's female stars – Angelina Jolie, Halle Berry and Cameron Diaz – was markedly different to the more androgynous, hard-bodied incarnation of the action heroine associated with the 1980s. The coupling of comedy and action is not new but a film like *Miss Congeniality's* (2000) staging of that comedy around the unlikely undercover role of tough FBI agent Gracie Hart (Sandra Bullock) as a beauty pageant contestant suggests the explicit engagement with and rejection of feminism. As Stasia neatly puts it, the film offers "its action hero significant physical freedoms and an independent mind only to rein them in with makeovers and men" (2007: 241–242).

Just as writers engaged with the tough male heroism of contemporary male action stars consider that these images have a wider cultural significance, feminist writers have been keen to map evolving ideas about women and gender through a discussion of action women. The formulation of female action heroes as in some way postfeminist has been a recurrent theme. The coupling of action and romantic comedy in *Mr & Mrs Smith* brings together violence with a genre that is firmly associated with media constructions of postfeminist woman. Angelina Jolie and Brad Pitt play a bored married couple, neither aware that the other is a top assassin. The central contradiction critics have repeatedly returned to is that between an evidently – for some excessively – sexualized filming of the female body on the one hand, and powerful images of female physical confidence and strength on the other.

Postmodern Action

Lisa Coulthard suggests that *Kill Bill* is both postfeminist and postmodern in the presentation of its vengeful, violent protagonist. Coulthard is not alone in describing *Kill Bill* as a postmodern action film. Indeed for some writers, action as a genre became increasingly self-conscious and stylized through the 1990s and the early twenty-first century. Writing in 2011, Lisa Purse succinctly summarizes the new normal: "Contemporary action cinema displays a self-conscious knowingness that proceeds from the popularisation of irony as a postmodern media practice in the previous decade" (2011: 7). Distancing techniques once used to critique or deconstruct generic norms are effectively "assimilated back into mainstream cinema," representing another stage in the evolution of action cinema.

What precisely do we mean when we talk about a postmodern action cinema? In part of course the designation is a way of pointing to a new stage of the genre, one characterized by a high degree of self-consciousness, as Purse suggests. There are at least four different aspects of action and adventure that the term *postmodern* helps us to capture: the sense of recycled culture or pastiche; the adoption of a self-conscious style; the widespread use of digital filmmaking and its implications for the portrayal of human action; a sense in which movies are responding to the experience of postmodernity.

Postmodern style is characterized by the incorporation of elements from past styles within contemporary genres, a decontextualized use of stars, signs and conventions from a diverse range of sources. Such juxtapositions of generic elements, periods or national film styles can be discordant or nostalgic in effect. Given the rich history of action and adventure cinema and its global manifestations, it is unsurprising that it tends to repeat itself. As A. O. Scott puts it in the *New York Times* review of *Inception* (2010), "movies, more often than not these days, are made out of other movies." All culture is recycled of course – and we should recall here that genre operates by processes of repetition and difference. Recycled culture is most evident when elements that are discordant are juxtaposed.

As we've seen, postmodern cinema is associated with a self-conscious or knowing address. Given action cinema's requirement for spectacle, the genre's self-consciousness is hardly surprising. Indeed action movies are often most self-conscious in their delivery of action sequences – inviting audiences to be amazed and to enjoy the spectacle. Scenes of spectacle are expanded in a number of ways, whether by multiple shots of the same event, the use of slow motion or via the simple expedient of holding characters in place to witness explosions or spectacular stunts in awe (their function to reinforce rather than direct the audiences gaze).

A self-conscious mode varies from the familiar one-liners of action heroes, wry commentary on the scale of events to a sense of seriousness that makes call on popular philosophy. An exemplary film of its moment, *The Matrix* features both of these types from Neo's "I know Kung Fu!" (the downloading of martial arts prowess a sharp contrast to the genre's typical insistence on an arduous and lengthy period of apprenticeship) to the portentous discourse of Morpheus. In the case of both the *Matrix* trilogy and *Inception*, at a narrative level it is more often the appearance of complexity rather than actual profundity at work. Both revolve around the illusion of appearances, the distinction between dreams and waking. And both make use of future world, science-fiction frameworks, staging spectacle effects sequences that play on the distortion of the image.

The fourth aspect worth considering here in more detail is the location of postmodern style as part of a broader set of responses to the experience of living with postmodernity. Theorists of early cinema have emphasized the nascent media as a response to the intensity of modernity. Jennifer Bean couples these questions explicitly to early action cinema and to the "trauma thrills" it offered, developing as it did in "overlap with a modernity in which the accelerated motion of transportation, technologies and that of optical devices linked together to create fundamental perceptual and psychic changes" (2004: 17). For Bean the early action cinema's exploitation of machines that break down – and the railway figures large in the adventure serials she considers – speaks to a sense of the "treacherous instability inherent to modernity's lust for precision and maximum power" (2004: 22). If urbanization, transportation systems and technologized warfare define modernity, postmodernity is characterized by a related and yet distinct cultural acceleration.

The intensely mediated character of contemporary culture, in which lives are lived in part online, and surveillance is embedded within commercial and state transactions, gives a particular resonance to the manipulation of the image that characterizes action cinema. Unsurprisingly, themes of surveillance are most apparent in crime and espionage action narratives; the monitoring of public space is rendered at times as reassuring (good people are watching) and at times a cause for concern – as in the dystopian *Minority Report* (2002), the tagline for which, "Everybody Runs …" encapsulates both the film's sinister tone and the promise of action more broadly.

CHAPTER 4

SILENT SPECTACLE AND CLASSICAL ADVENTURE: *THE THIEF OF BAGDAD* (1924) AND *THE ADVENTURES OF ROBIN HOOD* (1938)

While action emerges as a distinctive genre only in the 1980s, action genres are a longstanding feature of Hollywood film production, dating back to the very early days. The action films of the silent and classical cinema provide a useful reference point against which to situate more recent examples of film-making in the genre. As with subsequent decades, action and adventure films of these earlier periods were associated with particular stars: here, I focus on representative films of the 1920s and 1930s that starred Douglas Fairbanks (*The Thief of Bagdad*) and Errol Flynn (*The Adventures of Robin Hood*). Both titles were examples of high profile, prestige productions. They made use of elaborate sets and the latest technical innovations (*The Adventures of Robin Hood* was a high profile Technicolor production, for instance). Some of the issues raised by these films have remained important for critical perspectives

The Hollywood Action and Adventure Film, First Edition. Yvonne Tasker.
© 2015 John Wiley & Sons, Inc. Published 2015 by John Wiley & Sons, Inc.

on the genre: what are the modes of analysis best suited to spectacular forms of cinema? How should popular films, and action-oriented films in particular, be situated in relation to political and cultural themes of the day?

Adventure Spectacle in Silent Hollywood: The Thief of Bagdad (1924)

As the silent cinema reached maturity in the USA, Douglas Fairbanks established himself as one of the most remarkable and successful action stars of the period. From his success with *The Mark of Zorro* (1920), Fairbanks starred in and produced a series of often costly spectacles that showcased his athleticism and physical exuberance as well as proving commercial successes. Films such as *Robin Hood* (1922), *The Thief of Bagdad* (1924) and the experimental two-strip Technicolor production *The Black Pirate* (1926) set a high bar for adventure cinema while innovating in a number of areas of film production and set design.

Fairbanks was known for and defined by his physicality, in many ways prefiguring the action stars of later decades. Remarking on his "aesthetic of 'constant motion,'" Heather Addison suggests that "Fairbanks's agility made him uniquely qualified to exploit the possibilities of cinema as a *moving* medium" (2002: 28). She cites Fairbanks' own pronouncements (or those that were attributed to him at least), which underline his status as exemplar of physical culture, seeking to foreground what seems to be a characteristically American association between physical activity and moral worth:

> This system of ours – the universe – is founded on motion …
> All men walk, but the man who walks fastest is the one most apt to be noticed. Keep active, be enthusiastic, keep moving in mind and body. Activity is a synonym for health, and with health plus enthusiasm, wealth is just around the corner. (2002: 28)

That message of achievement through sheer exertion underpins both the cinematic pleasures and the expressly moral message of *The Thief of Bagdad*.

Reputedly the most expensive film made in Hollywood up to that point, *The Thief of Bagdad* deploys an elaborate fantastical frame for its spectacle, at the heart of which is a lesson on honesty and hard work (rather than wealth) as the route to happiness. Fairbanks plays Ahmed, a thief who resides under the city, stealing whatever takes his eye. When he falls in love with the daughter of the Caliph of Bagdad (Julanne Johnston), the thief at first plans to steal her; she is an object to be possessed like the money and food he boldly takes in the opening scenes. Yet Ahmed's sentiment – "What I want – I take!" – is clearly framed as selfish and immoral, prefiguring the charismatic gangster of the 1930s. The same words are spoken by the villainous Mongol Prince, Cham Shang (played by renowned Japanese actor Sojin Kamiyama), a parallel that makes clear the need for Ahmed to change. That change, triggered by desire for the Princess, will be achieved through the body in action, a narrative trajectory in line with the philosophy of virtuous exercise sketched previously.

Blagging his way into the palace in stolen clothes with the intention of abducting the Princess, ultimately Ahmed finds himself unable to carry through his plan. He has already won her heart – though the three princely suitors with whom he is compared do not pose much competition – but once he in turn is smitten, Ahmed confesses his true identity, insisting that he is reformed following their embrace ("The evil in me died"). Unmasked, Ahmed is flogged, echoing an earlier scene in which the hero pays horrified witness to the public flogging of a thief in the marketplace. The Princess intervenes to save Ahmed's life, bribing the guards to eject him from the palace rather than be torn apart by a giant ape (menacingly pictured) as they are instructed. She further stalls for time by setting her remaining suitors a seven month quest – she will marry whoever finds the rarest treasure. Thrown out onto the street, Ahmed seeks the help of a holy man and embarks on his own quest to make himself a Prince.

While the sets in the Bagdad scenes and indeed those in the palace are extraordinary in their scale, it is the quest sequences that *The Thief of Bagdad* deploys its most impressive effects; Ahmed faces a series of obstacles and opponents as he follows the path that leads from the "Mountains of Dread Adventure." The talents that served him as a thief – speed, bravery and agility – are allied to a new determination as he leaps across the Valley of Fire, slays a dragon in the Valley of the

Monsters and overcomes both a monstrous spider and the lure of mermaids under the Midnight Sea. These scenes of daring and bravery are contrasted with the actions of the three Princes, who rely on their servants and slaves to secure the treasures that they hope will win the Princess: one a flying carpet, the second a crystal ball and the third a golden apple that is capable of restoring life. All three exhibit negative qualities in acquiring these treasures, being both dishonest and indifferent to the lives of ordinary people.

On his quest Ahmed shows bravery, being rewarded with the aid of a winged horse that transports him through the clouds. The horse is featured in the film's poster, caught in an image of airborne dynamism, Fairbanks himself leaning forward intently. Guided by the horse to a domed structure in the sky, Ahmed secures a magic chest and cloak of invisibility. The chest's contents grant wishes: Ahmed transforms his rags into fine clothes, summons a horse and races to Bagdad. Ultimately the chest enables him to call forth an army to save the Princess and her father from the Mongol soldiers who have overrun Bagdad. Riding around the city, Ahmed produces thousands of magical soldiers as though he were sowing crops, the men appearing with puffs of smoke, their uniforms and banners glowing white. This is the climax of the film, offering the spectacle of an enormous cast of extras against the backdrop of the studio city and palace. Ahmed's magical assistance operates as an extension of his earlier thief persona – in the first part of the film he takes advantage of the call to prayers to steal a magical rope that he uses to scale the walls of the palace. Here, he besieges the whole city, an emphatic statement of his boldness that is visualized through the body in motion.

The Thief of Bagdad displays the cost of its production in both the mega-set of Bagdad and the spectacular action sequences that depict the quest. A striking aspect of both the city scenes and the quest through the Valley of the Monsters is that Fairbanks is frequently dwarfed by the sets. The marketplace, mosque and palace sets all tower above the human actors, while during the quest scenes Ahmed is pictured as a small figure against the challenges and creatures that he must face, not least the mermaid's cavernous palace into which he is almost seduced. As much as Fairbanks is a small figure in the scene, he differs from any other character in his ability to traverse the image from bottom to top with rapidity and grace. No other character crosses space in the way that Fairbanks' Ahmed does. Even in the shots of the three Princes sat on the magic carpet, their movement is strictly horizontal, never conveying the same freedom associated with Ahmed who is seen scaling the walls of the palace, using a sash of fabric to sail up to a balcony. In Fairbanks' adventure films, the hero is defined by precisely such freedom of movement as Ahmed exhibits, as well as an extraordinary energy. The only comparison in terms of the hero's opponents is a striking shot that depicts the Mongol Prince's soldiers scaling the walls of the palace – their massed ranks advance together in formation. Shot from above, the soldiers' uniforms form an abstract pattern, their movements never deviating from their ordered ranks.

The Thief of Bagdad was promoted as an event – a vast and vastly expansive production that underlines the association, familiar to modern audiences, between action and adventure and a cinema of superlatives. Promotional materials emphasized the scale of activity involved in the production and the grandeur of the resultant film's achievements, whether in sets "It took three wagon-loads of kelp for the undersea scenes" to the star's exertion "Jumping across abysses of fire, in whose yawning depths are beds of molten lava, is one of Douglas Fairbanks' simple little adventures in *Thief of Bagdad*." Directed by Raoul Walsh, the film extends and draws out the exotic or fantastic dimensions of the spectacle staged around Fairbanks in earlier films such as *Robin Hood*. *Thief* is an epic fairytale film featuring extravagant sets and breathtaking choreography. Fairbanks biographer John Tibbets cites contemporary poet and critic Vachel Lindsay for whom "the spectacular sweeping staircases were themselves 'actors in the grand manner'" (1996: 52). This formulation of the sets as more than background to the action is fundamental to much adventure cinema.

The Thief of Bagdad employs a number of tropes familiar to contemporary viewers of action cinema: the physical humiliation and subsequent triumph of the hero, feats of male athleticism and personal endeavor. As Gaylyn Studlar has persuasively argued, Fairbanks' star persona was characterized by a boyish masculinity that she relates to the contemporary culture's complex and evolving ideas about what it was to be a man. Fairbanks is both a comic and an athletic performer in his adventure titles, exemplifying this boyish man. *The Thief of Bagdad* follows Fairbanks' Ahmed from life as a thief on the streets of Bagdad, an amoral figure who takes what he wants, through the various adventures that end in his redemption through love and heroism; once again then the Fairbanks hero matures from an irresponsible boyish hero to a romantic hero.

While the film's press book materials celebrated "A Cast Of All Nations" (claiming that the film's cast "represents every country in the world, with the exception of Siam and Greenland"), it also describes star Fairbanks as exceptional within the cast as "a full-blooded, one hundred per cent American." The white American hero and the biggest male star of his day plays a Bagdad thief in an Arabian Nights fantasy: *The Thief of Bagdad* is immersed in the racial hierarchies and stereotypes in adventure cinema of the period, many of which, as we will see would continue (albeit modified) for decades to come.

The world serves as a backdrop for the adventures of the western/American hero with other cultures sketched in broad terms, and racial others confined to comic or villainous stereotypes. As Ziauddin Sardar and Merryl Wyn Davies write: "This was an Orient that could be dreamed, visited and possessed as past, present or future and yet would always be the same" (2010: 244). In a manner distinct from the Western or the jungle adventure films discussed in Chapter 2, *The Thief of Bagdad* employs an Orientalist imagery that, according to contemporary accounts, was fully exploited in the promotion of the film as exotic spectacle. *Thief* opened at Grauman's Egyptian Theatre, transforming a "whole section of Hollywood into a sort of Arabian night's fantasy in itself" (Karnes, 1986: 599). A contemporary report described Grauman's theatrical Prologue as "an attraction in itself," involving "more than one hundred players" and including "novelties such as a magician producing a dancer from a basket."[1] More than a promotional strategy, Orientalist pastiche operates as an important element of the film's aesthetic. *Thief* offers a wildly generalized Arabian world, an opulent spectacle peopled by actors from diverse nationalities. For John Eisele, *Thief* uses the escapist fantasy of the "Arabian Nights subgenre" to offer "American audiences, full of first- and second-generation immigrants" (2002: 81) a morality tale on social advancement.

---

[1] *Illustrated Daily News*, September 21st, 1924, Mary Pickford Papers, Margaret Herrick Library.

PLATE 4.1 Orientalist spectacle: *The Thief of Bagdad* stages its adventure against a fantasy backdrop (1924, directed by Raoul Walsh and produced by Douglas Fairbanks Pictures).

Gaylyn Studlar outlines some of the influences and cultural forms reworked by Fairbanks here. She writes: "In keeping with his aesthetic experiments of the 1920s, Fairbanks in *The Thief of Bagdad* exploits the sensuous textures of the Orient often evoked in German costume films such as *The Loves of Pharaoh* and *One Arabian Night*. Through costume design and other elements of *mise-en-scéne*, Fairbank's film imitates the look of the Ballets Russes' scenic design and the star imitates, in his highly physical movement, the modernist ballet techniques associated with Serge Diaghilev's controversial ballets" (1996: 87). That the film's Oriental themes are borrowed from German cinema is quite in keeping with the tone of the film, its composite, transcultural character.

The fantastic elements of the film are consistently foregrounded, via the dreamlike imagery of another time/place. The opening inter-title announces Bagdad, "dream city of the Ancient East", as the film's setting. The opening shot reveals a fantastic, bustling city scene, closing in via two cuts to Fairbanks' thief sprawled in seeming sleep. Ahmed is lovingly introduced to the audience; lying prone on a fountain, he forms a deceptively languid figure evocative of Orientalist stereotypes.

PLATE 4.2 Ahmed (Fairbanks) is integrated into *The Thief of Bagdad's* spectacle via costume, movement and gesture.

That repose is rapidly revealed as an impersonation, one designed to facilitate crime, as the seemingly sleepy Ahmed picks the pocket of a merchant who has stopped for water. His antics as a thief lead to comically inflected chase sequences in the early portion of the film, while his subsequent attempt to win the hand of the Princess leads him on an epic and physically challenging quest confronting fantastical creatures and villainous opponents.

Rudolph Valentino's successful desert romance films *The Sheik* (1921) and its sequel *Son of the Sheik* (1926) provide a contemporary reference point for Fairbanks' in some ways atypical role in *Thief* (the film certainly failed to match the commercial successes of Fairbanks' other 1920s adventures). Valentino's hero trades openly on associations between Arabian culture and sexuality. Fairbanks, prone to chest-beating and large gestures is never a figure of mystery in *The Thief of Bagdad* but rather a man of action. The opening shots aside, Fairbanks seems to be constantly in motion in *The Thief of Bagdad*, and while his character is the subject of a transformation narrative there is no change in his performance style that foregrounds action consistently.

The Thief of Bagdad is also notable for Anna May Wong's charismatic supporting role as the princesses' treacherous Mongol Slave. Although Wong became the first Chinese-American movie star, she was repeatedly frustrated by the stereotypical roles she was offered in Hollywood. In *The Thief of Bagdad*, her movements echoing stylized dance poses, she is contrasted to the Princesses loyal female servants who share her anxieties as the three suitors arrive at the Palace. The Mongol Prince, she tells them, "chills my blood with fear;" Wong's slave will attempt to assist him to win the Princess and the city through the course of the film, poisoning her at the Prince's instruction. Indeed in a strikingly composed shot she will reveal the Princesses to Sinjo's Mongol Prince, pulling aside a secret panel so that he may spy on her from above. In both her costume – which is elaborate and yet revealing – and her treacherous actions, the Slave character is opposed to the Princess in moral terms that are codified through race. That codification, which the cinema did not invent but certainly perpetuated, would persist in action and adventure genres for decades to come.

The Thief of Bagdad is not an historical adventure in Taves' sense of the term; its location both geographically and temporally is fantastic, an Orient that is a site of magical objects and impossible creatures. The film's spectacular sets, innovative effects and vast cast, along with its star's now familiar athleticism, establishes the association between adventure and prestige productions in the silent cinema. While its performances are overly drawn against contemporary styles of acting, many of the elements of the modern adventure film are clearly on display in *The Thief of Bagdad* and Douglas Fairbanks' other – less stylized – swashbucklers.

Classical Adventure: The Adventures of Robin Hood (1938)

Through the 1920s and 1930s adventure cinema of various types became a staple of American cinema with the setting of Merrie England and the folkloric figure of Robin Hood regularly portrayed on screen. In their assessment of the swashbuckler, which they also call "costume action," Higham and Greenberg write:

> ...the prototype of every swashbuckler of the era can be found in *The Adventures of Robin Hood* and [Errol] Flynn's other Thirties

films, mostly directed by Curtiz. They established a pattern, created a form, perfected a style that Fairbanks Senior had introduced to the cinema in the silent period. (1968: 124)

That formulation of an athletic performance style created by Fairbanks and taken up by a new star, the "lithe, athletic, quick and graceful" Flynn, is a common theme of historical accounts of the adventure cinema. These connections, while they may overlook the differences between Fairbanks and Flynn, work to emphasize the centrality of the star body and the convincing delivery of the action hero's diverse physical talents – from scaling walls and descending curtains/ropes, to swordplay, archery and other forms of combat. The physicality of the action-adventure star, that is, has been of central importance to the genre for decades.

In this context of a generic star legacy, it is worth briefly mentioning Douglas Fairbanks' *Robin Hood* (1922) – at the time the most expensive Hollywood production to date costing some $1.5 million – before moving to *The Adventures of Robin Hood*. Contemporary reviewers of the latter certainly compared the two. The design of Nottingham's castle in the Flynn version clearly echoes that of the 1922 film; not least via the curved stone staircase that winds around a central column and forms one of the locations in which the final fight between Robin and Basil Rathbone's Gisbourne takes place. In contrast to Flynn's Robin of Loxley, as the Earl of Huntingdon in his *Robin Hood* (1922) Fairbanks is comically afraid of and besieged by women after his victory at the tournament. It is only when his capacity for action is required – he intervenes to save Lady Marion (Enid Bennett) from Prince John's unwelcome attentions – that Huntingdon sets aside his shyness and is drawn into romance. Over an hour of the film will pass before Fairbanks' Huntingdon is reinvented as the outlaw hero.

As Robin, Fairbanks exudes good-humor and freedom; the film stages a pursuit of John's men around the castle that is effectively played as both comic (with slapstick elements) and thrilling, a combination of violence and humor that remains an element of action adventure traditions. Robin slides down the huge curtains that drape the walls, outwitting the massed guards. While the castle pursuit scene celebrates Robin's virtuosity and athleticism, the film's forest scenes celebrate men's martial brotherhood in generically familiar terms – for example, with an informal archery contest between Robin and Will Scarlet. *Robin Hood* employs a dynamic sense of character movement against the background of its monumental sets. The film juxtaposes scenes conveying the immense scale of the buildings and the large numbers of men moving around these sets, with the intimacy of romantic and fight scenes involving the central couple and the central antagonists respectively. Action was important for the Flynn version, with Michael Curtiz reputedly brought in as director after William Keighley in part for his skills in this aspect of filmmaking.[2] Such an awareness within the industry of the value of action sequences, and of the skills involved in getting this right is worth underlining. Both the ability to shoot action in a visually exciting manner and the ability to integrate these sequences into the narrative are vital.

Such dynamism would come to define the adventure cinema of classical Hollywood. Indeed in the 1938 rendition of the Robin Hood legend, the hero's fluid, graceful energy of movement comes to stand for his growing moral authority. As Ina Rae Hark observes, "Robin and his men are portrayed in natural surroundings and are character-ized by spontaneity of action and unrestrained motion; they generally create a dynamic mass within the frame" (1976: 7). Hark contrasts this fluidity to the presentation of the Normans in the film, consistently "rigid and artificial," organized into rows and characterized by unyielding symmetry. "In short," writes Hark, "the Normans are con-trolled by an inflexible protocol, visually expressed through geomet-rical symmetry, which is all the more deadly because it masks sadism and greed" (1976: 9). This expressive composition reaches back to Eisenstein's Odessa Steps sequence of *Battleship Potemkin* (1925). In the vein of Hollywood action and adventure heroes to come, Flynn's Robin Hood is able to adapt to his environment, climbing up vines, leaping onto horses and using anything that comes to hand in a fight. Both Robin's athleticism and his proximity to the people facilitate his

[2] Tony Thomas writes that following their viewing of Keighley's footage, including the fight between Robin and Little John, Warner's "decided his approach was too lyrical and that what was needed was more exciting and more driving direction" (1976: 77). Nollen notes additionally that under Keighley the production had gone over schedule and over budget (1999: 107).

escape from Sir Guy as the men of Sherwood join the crowds gathered to watch his public hanging.

A Technicolor epic, *The Adventures of Robin Hood* was nominated for Best Picture, securing the Academy Awards for art direction, film editing and original score. Such recognition for technical accomplishment would come to characterize action and adventure films, a genre in which the emphasis on visual spectacle meant experimentation with the possibilities of the medium. The film made use of both sets and location work, employing the forest at Chico, California as Sherwood. Though in common with other adventure films the costumes and violence are stylized, the commitment to getting details correct in elements of weaponry was extensive, and indeed the various displays of archery and swordsmanship were regarded as useful marketing devices for the film. Bernard McConville's gloss on his initial 1936 treatment and subsequent script – which went through numerous revisions at Warner's – emphasized the importance of archery as a source of spectacle within the movie and as a marketing point. Exhibitors would be advised to target boy scouts and the "large number of girl students in schools and universities who follow archery as a sport."[3]

The Adventures of Robin Hood pits Errol Flynn's Robin against Basil Rathbone's Sheriff of Nottingham with Claude Rains as Prince John and Olivia de Havilland as Marion. If *The Thief of Bagdad* exemplifies the fantastic possibilities of prestige adventure filmmaking in the silent era, *The Adventures of Robin Hood* is an exemplary adventure narrative of the classical period. The film couples lavish spectacle – scenes of pursuit, capture and escape, an archery contest and playful contests of staff and swordsman ship between the outlaws – and the elaborate sets these scenes required, with broad political themes of liberation and freedom from oppression. In the immediate run-up to the outbreak of war in Europe, the film offered – in line with other Warner's productions – as explicit a condemnation of authoritarian regimes as was perhaps possible at the time (Hollywood eschewed politics, espousing the neutrality of the US in relation to Europe and its conflicts).

In its alignment with oppressed Saxons against Normans *The Adventures of Robin Hood* exploits the political impulses that Taves sees

---

[3] Screen Play Treatment by Bernard McConville, March 5th 1936, Script files held in Margaret Herrick Library.

as central to the historical adventure, without ever needing to touch on the complexities of power and oppression within the US itself. Even tackling religion too directly was felt to be risky – thus Friar Tuck is a martial more than a religious hero (a "dangerous swordsman" remarks Little John). Hark reads the tale as both a commentary on the rise of fascism in Europe and as a reflection on the recent history of the United States. Prince John's concern is as much with taxation as with seizing the throne of England. And as Hark observes, "the root of John's tyranny is so obviously monetary" that "nominally a Prince, John behaves much more like a corruptible minor bureaucrat or shady financier" (1976: 4). She frames her remarks in the context of Jack Warner's well-known advocacy for Roosevelt: "Whether Robin Hood represents a retrospective look at America's emergence from economic disorder or a prophetic glance at World War II, the heroes Robin and Richard in large part stand in for Franklin Roosevelt" (1976: 6).

Social differences of class and ethnicity structure the conflict in Robin Hood, differences between Norman and Saxon that are constructed as cultural rather than racial. Indeed the racial politics of the segregated United States did not register in adventure films, with their historically removed settings. Notably one of the writers who worked on the script saw a parallel, referring in his notes to the Norman's "Jim Crow" highway laws, designed by the Normans to keep the Saxons in their place."[4] In the notes accompanying McConville's 1936 treatment, this version of Robin is described as an "*ideal hero*," decidedly "*not* a highway robber, *but an emancipator*."[5]

As numerous scholars have noted, the appeal of the romantic Robin Hood figure that originates with Sir Walter Scott's *Ivanhoe* (1820) is his ability to encapsulate both rebellion against unjust authority (his battles with Prince John, Guy of Gisbourne and the Sheriff of Nottingham) and loyalty to the state (to the English people, but most particularly to King Richard). A royalist rebel, Robin performs a similar function to rogue cops in later action scenarios: he

---

[4] Working outline by Philip Dunne, March 25th 1935, Script Files held in Margaret Herrick Library.
[5] Screen Play Treatment by Bernard McConville, March 5th 1936, Script files held in Margaret Herrick Library. Emphasis in original.

PLATE 4.3 The arrival of the rebellious Robin Hood (Errol Flynn), bearing with him a royal deer, disrupts Prince John's banquet in *The Adventures of Robin Hood* (1938, directed by Michael Curtiz and William Keighley and produced by Warner Bros.).

represents authority and stability while challenging the powerful and the unjust systems they seek to impose. As a new kind of "English hero, highly masculine, deeply committed to nature," to quote Stephen Knight, Scott's Robin Hood is a yeoman rather than a member of the gentry (2006: 155). The film has it both ways, Sir Robin of Loxley is a Saxon noble who loses his lands and is knighted by the returned King Richard in the final scene. He is both a figure of established authority and a rebellious outlaw.

While politics has long been central to the different versions of Robin Hood and the specific context of late 1930s United States frames the Warner Bros. film, adventure presents the narrative of resistance to oppression in a particularly vivid and relatively simple manner. Conflict and violence are crucial elements here, and while the violence of the adventure film is, as we've seen, typically somewhat bloodless in character, *The Adventures of Robin Hood* nonetheless presents a more brutal imagery of violence. That brutality concerns the treatment of the Saxon people, the depiction of which was modified at the request of PCA.[6] The tyranny begins following the opening scene in which Prince John vows that Richard will not return, a spilled goblet of wine running red on the rug to underline his evil intent. Food is confiscated from a Saxon merchant. A holy man protests as a "freeborn" man is enslaved for refusing to send his men to work on Gisbourne's fields. Robin fires his first arrow in defense of Much, who will pledge service to him in gratitude. Robin's arrow is expertly targeted to disarm Guy of Gisbourne who is about to beat the man for killing one of the King's deer. The mounted Gisbourne towers over Much, in any case rather diminutive, the camera positioning emphasizing these differences of power and aligning us with the Saxon as a feisty figure in peril. Since Robin is also on horseback the two are established as equivalent figures in stature, their animosity continuing until the final set-piece duel between the two during the film's climactic battle in Nottingham Castle.

The Adventures of Robin Hood attempts to keep a balance between the depiction of violence and inferring the brutality of the Normans to keep within the bounds of censorship. In his rousing Sherwood speech to the men of the forest, Robin refers to Saxons blinded with hot irons; the camera moves across those who have assembled to hear him, at this point picking up a man with an eye-patch who nods, testifying to the violent treatment. This scene is followed by a title that tells how "Terror spread among the helpless Saxons who knew that resistance meant death." There follows a montage of oppression and defiance: a man close to death about to be flogged again, Robin's arrow killing the Norman soldier who gives the order; a Saxon about to be hanged begs for mercy, the dangling legs above showing that another has hung before him – a Norman soldier's cruel laughter is cut short by an arrow; an elderly man is chained up while soldiers destroy casks of wine, his daughter grabbed by a leering Norman soldier before an arrow strikes him in the back. These atrocities and the revenge exacted for them are in line with Robin's doctrine of

[6]   In a series of letters from September 1937 to January 1938 Joseph Breen cautions Warner on the overly "gruesome" or vivid depiction of tortures inflicted on the Saxons.

revolt, an eye for an eye, his vow to "fight to the death against our oppressors." Although he adopts what are in effect guerrilla tactics the hero is typically defined by his open and direct character: he is what he appears to be, directly waylaying those who pass through Sherwood, as when he confronts the disguised King Richard towards the end of the film.

These first victories for Robin and his men are followed by a more significant reversal for Prince John's forces as the men of Sherwood ambush a party led by the Sheriff of Nottingham and Guy of Gisbourne. Jumping down from above, swinging from vines there is something of the jungle adventure about the scene. The forest feast offers an inversion of the Norman banquet with its cold formality. The confrontation here is once more bloodless, though the violence of the conflict between Saxons and Normans frames the scenes. Indeed leading Marian away from the feast, Robin shows her a mortifying sight – fearful people who have had their homes burned, been beaten and starved: "tortured, eyes put out, tongues slit, ears hacked off – they come to me for protection" he tells her.

That contrast between violence as brutal and intense on one hand, light-hearted and amongst comic on the other persists through the film. Just as Much's romance with Marian's servant Besse provides a comic counterpoint to Robin and Marian's relationship, during the final battle – some four minutes in length – while Robin duels Sir Guy, Much is in the rafters of the Castle, lifting off helmets and cracking Norman heads from his vantage point. Meanwhile the duel is of an utterly different character, not only a display of violence and swordsmanship but elaborately filmed involving a mobile camera that captures the shadows of the two men as they fight, a mix of close-ups, medium and long shots that build tension. Once Sir Guy is defeated and falls from the steps, we see a shot of Robin pausing to look down and then a medium shot of the corpse, eyes open in a graphic image of death quite unlike the numerous Norman soldiers who fall to arrows or to missiles.

The personal development of the hero turns in *The Adventures of Robin Hood* on politics and romance; the first makes Robin an outlaw, the second provides a strong focus for the hero's desire. The third of the eight films in which Flynn and de Havilland co-starred, their relationship was an important promotional point alongside the spectacle and action sequences. In the early part of the film the two are portrayed as sparring; the tension between Norman Marian and Saxon Robin links the film's broader political themes with the romance narrative. The Saxons are simple and rather rough while the Normans are sophisticated but cruel. She is initially disdainful – "What a pity her manners don't match her looks" he remarks – and later judges him a "Saxon hedge robber." Yet Marian is clearly different from the other Normans – not only that she is brave and defiant: "I am afraid of nothing, least of all you," she tells Robin after her capture in Sherwood.

Robin's revelation of the misery endured by the Saxon people during the Sherwood scenes serves to break down differences between himself and Marian and to facilitate their relationship. Across the different treatments of the screenplay developed for Warner's the character of Marian is also adapted for the tastes of a modern audience. The pair are imagined in one version as "a couple of comrades" with both in Lincoln green. Marian is also envisaged as possessing fighting skills in line with the ambition to speak to female audience members: "Marion is no weak and timid girl, but a strong and nervy almost boyish athlete. She is a mad-cap by nature and that is the reason she understands and loves Robin Hood."[7] The vision of the pair living together in Sherwood Forest was eliminated from subsequent versions of the script – no doubt since it implied a sexual relationship outside marriage. The Lincoln green goes too, although Marian wears a green cloak when she goes to the men of Sherwood to seek their help in staging a daring escape for Robin.

Marian's independent spirit in *The Adventures of Robin Hood*, is rather different from the female leads in Douglas Fairbanks' adventure films. Though she does not fight directly, her lack of fear and her sense of justice make her and Robin well suited. She facilitates the daring rescue of Robin and opts to remain in the Castle to watch for treachery. Like Robin – who is captured when in disguise – Marian has little success in subterfuge. Ineffective at hiding her feelings or indeed concealing herself, she is apprehended almost immediately by Sir Guy.

[7] Screen Play Treatment by Bernard McConville, March 5th 1936, Script files held in Margaret Herrick Library.

Prince John declares that in 48 hours when he is made King he will order her execution: thus the situation is reversed and Robin must engineer Marian's rescue from the Castle.

Conclusion

The Thief of Bagdad and *The Adventures of Robin Hood* point to the centrality of action and adventure in Hollywood's silent and classical periods. These were expensive and prestigious productions. They required elaborate sets and not only showcased major stars but depended on these stars athleticism to carry the fictional world. These adventure films featured action sequences prominently. Additionally they underline the ideological and political aspects of such fantasy films, whether films are seen to advocate a particular position (*Robin Hood* as a pre-war argument for achieving freedom by force) or crystallize debates that will continue to be important in framing action and adventure cinema (the racial discourses at work in *The Thief of Bagdad*).

CHAPTER 5

WAR, VIOLENCE AND THE AMERICAN ACTION HERO: *SANDS OF IWO JIMA* (1949) AND *HELL IS FOR HEROES* (1962)

Although the war film is widely regarded as a genre in its own right, World War II and its cinematic representation is enormously significant for understanding the historical and thematic development of action and adventure traditions in Hollywood cinema. Along with the Western and crime thrillers or *film noir*, the war film operates as a key action genre through the 1940s to the 1960s. Featuring extensive scenes of combat, a focus on the male group and on themes of redemption through violence, the war film generates tropes that would become familiar elements within the action cinema that emerged as a distinctive genre in subsequent decades.

The conventions of the American war movie and the particular character of World War II combat film have been extensively and productively analyzed. Jeanine Basinger outlines the development of the form, identifying its first definitive articulation in *Bataan* (1943). Since

The Hollywood Action and Adventure Film, First Edition. Yvonne Tasker.
© 2015 John Wiley & Sons, Inc. Published 2015 by John Wiley & Sons, Inc.

my focus in this book is on action and adventure rather than the war movie as such, it is worth drawing out those "action" features identified by Basinger as significant aspects of the genre. Of the conventions Basinger elaborates, it is those concerning the characterization of the hero (and the team he leads) and the portrayal of combat that are most pertinent to the development of a recognizable action cinema in the decades to come. For example, Basinger suggests that the hero of the combat film typically has the responsibilities of leadership enforced on him in some way – his responsibilities are acquired rather than sought out. This convention prefigures the modern action hero who does not look for the violent and dangerous positions in which he finds himself (in *Die Hard 2*, McClane quips "we are just up to our neck in terrorists again John!"). Nonetheless in both war and action genres the hero is well suited to tackle these challenges when they arise.

In the combat sequences of the World War II film, Basinger identities a powerful and recognizable pattern: "A series of episodes occur which alternate in uneven patterns the contrasting forces of night and day, action and repose, safety and danger, combat and noncombat, comedy and tragedy, dialogue and action" (2002: 74). The tension of night in combat films, and the anticipation of attack is played out in both of the films discussed in this chapter – *Sands of Iwo Jima* (1949) and *Hell is for Heroes* (1962) – and will come to form a key convention of the action film. The underlying pattern, which contrasts stillness and movement, silence and sound, is employed across the range of action genres. Indeed this pattern of switching between action and release provides a formal framework within which the set-pieces of the action film enhance the spectacle offered. The convention by which not only a "climactic battle takes place," but "a learning or growth processes occurs" as part of that battle and its resolution are also familiar to modern viewers. Moreover, while war films of the Vietnam and post-Vietnam era were decidedly different in tone, the convention of the World War II combat film whereby an important military objective is identified and secured feeds many subsequent action films that stage the narrative of conflict in fantastic terms.

In considering the significance of the war film as part of Hollywood action and adventure, this chapter discusses two World War II films in detail that were both released well after the end of the war, in 1949 and 1962, both conclude with the death in combat of the male soldier hero (played by John Wayne and Steve McQueen, respectively), and both point to the emergence of two themes that would become increasingly significant in the action cinema: an increasing ambivalence towards authority and the characterization of heroes who are both violent and psychologically troubled or damaged. These films couple what Jeanine Basinger, with reference to *Battleground* (1949) and *Sands of Iwo Jima*, terms "the new realism, the old conventions, *and* a postwar message" (2002: 166).

As examples of what Thomas Doherty terms the "retrospective World War II film" (1999: 273), these movies present combat action to audiences at a little distance from the experience of the war itself – rather more so in the case of *Hell is for Heroes*, although in the early 1960s the Korean War was a more recent memory and the involvement of US troops in the Vietnam War – albeit not on the scale seen later in the decade – had already commenced. The retrospective war film inevitably adopts a different perspective than titles made during the war itself. In the decades following World War I for example, a number of well-known, emotionally powerful anti-war films such as *All Quiet on the Western Front* (1930) were made.

Though Doherty regards *Sands of Iwo Jima* as exemplifying "sanitized guts and glory" (1999: 272), it nonetheless features elements of a questioning relationship to authority rarely seen in films made during the war itself. Indeed Robert Eberwein positions *Sands of Iwo Jima* as one among a group of films of the late 1940s in which heroes are presented as "psychologically troubled men." For Eberwein such retrospective war films involved "complicated examinations of leadership and authority, issues that were not raised in combat films made during the war." (2010: 23) Such concerns are more explicit in *Hell is for Heroes*, perhaps in line with Steve McQueen's loner star image that would figure in the influential cop thriller *Bullitt* (1968).

In parallel with such a questioning stance, we see the sharper definition of an outsider masculinity associated strongly with violence and loss. The evocation of a male hero whose capacity for violence is both necessary to the formation or the maintenance of communities, yet simultaneously excludes him from full inclusion, has been explored at length in relation to the Western and the *noir* thriller as well as the war film; indeed the social anxieties associated with returning veterans has often been used to contextualize the violence and uncertainty of

American film noir for instance.[1] The action hero of subsequent decades would routinely be established as a man with a military past, experiences that testify to his strength, courage and abilities. This said, the status of the veteran as a figure of potential violence and danger can also be said to haunt action films, not least in the iconic 1980s action hero John Rambo, played by Sylvester Stallone.

As an action genre the war film is distinguished by a particular relationship to history. In depicting events that took place in living memory, or indeed on-going events, war films must manage carefully their representation of battle, death and national purpose.[2] *Bataan*, released in 1943 following the disastrous defeat of United States troops on the peninsula the year before is an extreme case perhaps. Indeed the film is well-known for its tight focus on events within the overall campaign and its effective evocation of individual bravery in the face of defeat. If wartime filmmaking frequently fulfils propagandistic purposes and is heavily monitored or censored (not to mention typically unpopular with audiences), post-war films must also manage the representation of events, particularly if military assistance is sought in the production.

Thus while historical authenticity might be an issue for the adventure cycle, as Taves argues, or plausible effects necessary for fantasy action adventure traditions, the war film is judged and discussed as realistic (or not) in a rather different way. The historical immediacy of war, the very opposite of the historical remove associated with much adventure cinema, and the presence of death and loss renders the genre particularly powerful. Questions of realism, or more precisely authenticity, come to form a major concern for the war movie: the authentic rendition of experience is used, for example, to justify the graphic representation of violent combat and death. Siegel regarded his film *Hell is for Heroes* as "extremely realistic" getting to the "sordid" character of war (Lovell, 1975: 56). The *New York Times* review of *Sands of Iwo Jima* remarked on its "savage realism" and "honesty."[3] For many

[1] See for example, Frank Krutnik's (1991) discussion of *The Blue Dahlia* and other "tough" thrillers featuring returning soldier heroes.

[2] Doherty cites a front page story in *Variety* in the year that *Sands* was released: "war proved no box office poison in 1949" (1999: 272).

[3] *Sands of Iwo Jima*, *New York Times*, December 31st, 1949.

contemporary critics there was a fine line between honesty and exploitation, with the discourse of realism operating across that line.

Combat scenes need to be staged in a manner that satisfies the desire for action while remaining respectful of the losses sustained in war (the portrayal of corpses is particularly charged). Moreover, the hero's capacity for violence is typically bound into the military as an institution: the recurrence of training narratives and sequences, as well as the insistence on discipline and rules all speak to the war movie as a representation of sanctioned violence. As we see throughout this study, however, action and adventure cinema typically favors maverick or outsider figures over those who represent institutions or authority in a more straightforward way. Moreover, the brutality and cynicism that begin to emerge in post-war films suggests a different perspective on martial heroism.

John Wayne, Outsider Masculinity and The Sands of Iwo Jima

Independently produced by Republic Pictures, the *Sands of Iwo Jima* is indicative of the ways in which the war movie had already begun to shift by the end of the 1940s. Contemporary reviewers emphasized what they regarded as the film's brutal realism in its depiction of violence and death. Indeed dialogue with the PCA and with the military turned on violence with a 1949 memo reminding the producers of the necessity to shoot combat scenes with discretion: "Here and in all of the other battle action, please avoid photographing scenes of excessive brutality or gruesomeness. This is important."[4]

According to Lawrence Suid, the film's genesis lay in Republic producer Edmund Grainger who took the title from a newspaper line and the inspiration for the film's climax from Joe Rosenthal's famous photograph of the raising of the flag at the top of Mount Surabachi: from its initial publication that image rapidly became iconic, securing a Pulitzer Prize for Rosenthal. Suid observes that Grainger "wanted *Sands of Iwo Jima* to be 'very realistic' and 'under no circumstances' did he want to 'make a Hollywood version of the Marine Corps'" (1978: 27).

[4]   PCA Memo, June 21 1949. Margaret Herrick Library

If the production was committed to a brutal realism in conveying war, it remained respectful of the Marines and of military culture. For the film's production team a commitment to represent the combat experience of the Marine Corps as authentically as possible was a stated goal, an ambition facilitated by the extensive support provided in equipment, men and so on. Suid records that director Allan Dwan "received use of a company of Marines who were available at all times to serve as background for the actors" (1978: 28).

Having a Marine advisor, Captain Leonard Fribourg, assigned at the pre-production stage enabled the producer, director and editor to "select combat footage which would later be matched with the recreated action" (Suid, 1978: 26). The final film made extensive and effective use of such footage, cutting between images of the squad about to land at Tawara and Iwo Jima and footage of shelling, landings and explosions. The *Motion Picture Daily* review picked up on this:

> Part of the footage is official. Most of it was staged at Camp Pendleton, Oceanside, Cal., with the full cooperation of the Marine Corps. Of the genuine footage, obviously there can be no doubt, but the rest of it is completely and authoritatively in the flavour of the real thing.[5]

As the *Daily* reviewer notes, the shift between the actual footage and the scenes filmed at Pendleton is apparent in the different quality of the stock. What particularly characterizes *Sands of Iwo Jima* is the effective integration of these scenes so that the links are both obvious and yet seamless, adding to the power of the film's extensive combat-action sequences. And of course as the *Daily* review also notes, these sequences also work to generate a sense of authenticity to the battle scenes, positioning the actors in the midst of events.

Now clearly a film that takes its title and climactic sequence from a photograph is invested in realism of a quite particular – and highly mediated – kind. In fact in many ways *Sands of Iwo Jima* exemplifies the World War II combat film formula, bringing together a mixed group of diverse (white) Americans who learn to work together as a team. Although the battles on Tawara and Iwo Jima provide the action

---

[5]   *Motion Picture Daily*, 14th December 1949

focus of the film, *Sands of Iwo Jima* centers on the charismatic figure of Sergeant Stryker – played by John Wayne – and his efforts to train a squad of Marines into a "sound fighting unit" (as one of the men expresses it in his voiceover). "I'm gonna get the job done," snarls Stryker in his address to the squad on first meeting – and so he does. The generational tension between Stryker as trainer/father figure and his reluctant squad is ultimately resolved through combat; both Pete Conway (John Agar) and Al Thomas (Forrest Tucker), though initially hostile, come to understand the value of the lessons that Stryker has drilled into them.

Stryker's toughness is strongly resented, and though he ultimately comes to be respected by the men he leads, for the majority of the film he is isolated from them, a figure apart. Wayne plays Stryker as a deeply troubled man, "lonely, disoriented" (Basinger, 2002: 169). Doherty evocatively summarizes the role: "Alcoholic, divorced, insubordinate, Sergeant Stryker is among the walking wounded; he charges an enemy machinegun nest because he has so little to lose" (1999: 273). It is revealed early in the film that his wife has left him five years previously, taking their son, now 10 years-old, with whom Stryker has no contact. This loss of family shapes the Sergeant's tough yet melancholy persona – an unfinished letter to his son in which he describes himself as having "been a failure in many ways" will be read aloud by Thomas following Stryker's death.

In common with many other war films, *Sands of Iwo Jima* foregrounds themes of personal transformation via the familiar conventions of the training camp movie. Thomas learns the cost of negligence when his act of stopping for coffee rather than taking ammunition straight back to his comrades leads to one of them being killed. Conway learns that military masculinity is required in times of war, reconciling himself to his Marine father's memory. Indeed in the closing moments of the film – having recently become a father himself – Conway now steps up to the part vacated by Stryker, swallowing his emotion to call out: "Alright, saddle up! Let's get back in the war!"

Stryker himself is changed not through combat – he has already proved himself in this arena – but through an encounter during a period of liberty in Honolulu. Here he meets Mary who invites him back to her rooms for a drink. Stryker gives her money to buy alcohol and in her absence discovers an infant child in a back room. On her return Mary observes: "There are a lot tougher ways of making a living than going to war." The implication of Mary's status as a prostitute was the single element of the script that PCA officials objected to most vigorously, initiating a lengthy chain of correspondence on the matter. Ultimately a compromise was reached over various phone calls with Breen, with an agreement to shoot the scene as written before submitting it for approval; this was accepted with strong warnings that the film wouldn't be passed if the implication that Mary is a prostitute remains.[6] The significance of this exchange – aside from the prurience of the PCA – is the centrality of the scene in Stryker's personal development. The encounter draws him out of his self-pity and signals a reengagement with the world.

Four years after the end of World War II and only one year before the United States would be at war once again in Korea, *Sands of Iwo Jima* aims to balance celebratory and realist impulses. In doing so it

PLATE 5.1 Sgt Stryker (John Wayne) relaxes with his men immediately before his shocking death in *Sands of Iwo Jima*. The loss of the male hero temporarily disrupts the film's triumphal conclusion (1949, directed by Allan Dwan and produced by Republic Pictures (I)).

[6] Letter from Joseph Breen, August 19 1949, PCA file, Margaret Herrick Library

deploys a number of character types and conventions that remain familiar within contemporary action cinema. The film's celebratory discourse is apparent – *Sands of Iwo Jima* ends with the image it works towards and which was widely used in promotional images for the film, that of the flag-raising on Mount Surabachi. The evocation of this famous image of victory, later unpicked in Clint Eastwood's *Flags of our Fathers* (2006) involves the use of the three surviving flag-raisers (Wayne hands them the flag) as well as other military personnel playing themselves.

Yet in *Sands* that stirring imagery follows immediately on from the shocking scene of Stryker's death, a death that is not a result of some heroic feat but which occurs randomly as he sits relaxing with his men, about to smoke a cigarette ("I never felt so good in my life"). For Basinger the moment, "one of the most shocking and heart-breaking moments in all the combat films," recalls anti-war classic, *All Quiet on the Western Front* (2002: 167). And yet *Sands of Iwo Jima* cannot really be described as an anti-war film since it never seriously questions the necessity of the campaigns depicted. The *Hollywood Reporter* proclaimed "War is not a pleasant thing to contemplate, but if another is to be prevented, recollection is important." The review adds: "When a film like this one [*Sands of Iwo Jima*] issues from Hollywood it is obvious that the picture industry is not shirking its responsibilities."[7] Such claims say as much about the perceived need to justify the pleasurable violence of Hollywood cinema – a core component of the action genre – as they do about the significance of the war film.

Doherty contrasts the "textual caution" so evident in *Sands of Iwo Jima* with the film's gung-ho publicity and promotion: "The marketing campaign for *Sands of Iwo Jima*, rereleased in 1954 and circulating throughout the 1950s, is all upbeat glorification." For Doherty the celebratory discourse of the film's promotion, at least on rerelease after the end of the Korean War was directly addressed to what was increasingly regarded as Hollywood's preferred audience: "Nourishing sweet Homeric dreams and luxuriating in the manly compensations of combat, trailers and one-sheet advertisements took dead aim at the teenage male temperament" (1999: 274). Such connections between

---

[7]   *Hollywood Reporter*, December 14th 1949

film promotion and military recruitment would be a recurrent feature of the American action cinema, with *Top Gun* (1986) reputedly boosting interest in the Navy.

Writing of *Sands of Iwo Jima*, Basinger argues that the "death of John Wayne helps to mark the film's departure from the earlier wave of combat films" (2002: 152). Wayne was a star associated with a number of action genres, most obviously the Western but also the war movie and adventure cinema. Indeed by the late 1940s when *Sands of Iwo Jima* was released – and for which he received an Oscar nomination – Wayne was establishing himself within war movies while remaining an iconic figure of the Western. His repeated call to his men to "Saddle Up!" nicely couples the two. Wayne's imposing physical presence was a feature of his films as of his star persona; his size, stoicism and conservatism are somewhat at odds with the action hero, defined as s/he is by mobility and urgency (think of the athleticism of Fairbanks). The sudden, unexpected death of the character played by the iconic Wayne speaks powerfully then to the violence of war evoked throughout the film by its powerful battle scenes and careful use of actual footage.

Hell is for Heroes: Violence, Heroism and the "Dirty" War Films of the 1960s

Some 13 years after *Sands of Iwo Jima*, *Hell is for Heroes* (directed by Don Siegel) showcases an even darker presentation of the violence of war and the nihilistic figure of the hero played by Steve McQueen. In celebrating teamwork and individual heroism yet portraying that heroism as effectively unsupported by military authorities, the film prefigures the tone of many subsequent action films.

Hell is for Heroes is frequently described as an uncompromising war film. As with *Sands of Iwo Jima*, reviewer responses to *Hell is for Heroes* foregrounded realism as a context for the film's violence. The opening credits consist of a series of frozen action images from the film, the only moving image an explosion, an action image that accompanies the title credit. This combination of a documentary photography quality with the spectacle of explosion captures the different dimensions of *Hell is for Heroes*. The *Hollywood Reporter* praised the film in terms of "a

PLATE 5.2 The battle scenes in *Hell is for Heroes* foreground explosive action spectacle; heroism is framed less by themes of patriotic purpose than those of violence and death (1962, directed by Don Siegel and produced by Paramount Pictures).

grim theme realistically handled."[8] *Variety* described the movie as "hard-hitting," suggesting that the emphasis on action would appeal to male viewers:

> The Paramount release should be a popular attraction with male audiences and filmgoers who prefer an emphasis an explosive, nerve-shattering action in their war dramas. Exploited as a raw, turbulent and yet intimate depiction of the ironic patterns of combat behaviour, as enacted by a company of youthful, virile and reliable actors, the film might earn its stripes in the action market.[9]

The equation evoked here between action, violence and masculinity represents familiar territory for contemporary audiences.

Steve McQueen's star persona was built on a sense of restless urgency, a maverick, countercultural distance from authority and an association above all with speed (the fast draw, his passion for racing).

[8] *The Hollywood Reporter*, May 23rd 1962
[9] *Variety*, May 21st 1962

PLATE 5.3 Reese (Steve McQueen) isolates himself from the rest of the squad; reluctant to return home, *Hell is for Heroes* pictures him as a figure of violence suited for war.

Like fellow 1960s action star Clint Eastwood, McQueen came to prominence in a television Western, also securing his first significant box office success in a Western, *The Magnificent Seven* (1960). McQueen's Reese is introduced as a latecomer to the squad in *Hell is for Heroes*, joining them as they are gathered at a rest area near the Siegfried Line. Rebuffing conversation, Reese exchanges a faint smile with only Sgt Pike (Fess Parker). Otherwise he remains a terse, silent figure in contrast to the squad's banter and camaraderie. The troops gather in a derelict church; Reese is told the town is off limits but heads for the local bar anyway, a small rebellion that underlines his misfit status.

Paramount's Press Book for *Hell is for Heroes* attribute to McQueen a characterization of the film as an adult war drama: "We give you a hero and don't depict him as handsome and wholesome and full of only estimable qualities" the actor explained.

We tell you there are brave men in this world who are also bums. I think audiences will appreciate our determination to do away with the old formula stuff that the good fellows wear the white and the bad guys can always be detected because theirs are black.

McQueen's character Reese is brave, professional and yet also impersonal, even inhuman, a figure who exemplifies the violence of war. The prospect of being shipped home sends Reese into dark gloom, his energy returning when Pike tells him that they are instead going back into combat.

Hell is for Heroes is not alone in its blurring of the figure of the hero in time of war. As discussed in Chapter 2, the "dirty war movie" demonstrates both an historical distance from World War II and a proximity to conflicts such as the Korean and Vietnam Wars. Aldrich's *The Dirty Dozen* centers on a team of criminals enlisted by military authorities to a brutal mission; from its opening scene with a visceral image of a young soldier being hung to the climactic torching of the chateau in which German officers and their female companions are trapped suggests a vicious inflection of the violence of war. Tony Williams describes *The Dirty Dozen* as

> an extremely ambivalent film. It never delivers any explicitly educational position but instead represents the supposed good war as an ugly arena of violence in which everyone, including fictional characters and audiences, ends up tarnished and corrupted by participating (voyeuristically or not) in the spectacular bloodshed of a supposedly "good cause." (2004: 347)

Hell is for Heroes centers too on a mission the value of which is questionable. The squad of six men must hold a section of the line, convincing the German forces they face that they are present in much larger numbers. Enlisting the help of Driscoll, an army typist who inadvertently finds himself in combat, the men show their ingenuity: they rig Driscoll's jeep to sound like a tank, running it up and down the line to give the impression of greater numbers; the Lieutenant himself (played by Bob Newhart) is employed to fake reports to HQ in which he bemoans the quality of the vichyssoise. Yet if these scenes are reminiscent of a heist movie, the comic (or at least surreal) undertone is tempered by McQueen's mechanical demeanor and by the increasing darkness and violence of the combat. Henshaw (James Coburn), a bespectacled soldier, initially portrayed as endearingly obsessed with machinery, shifts into steely mode, using a flamethrower to kill a German soldier, the latter's agonized screams matched by

Henshaw himself who screams aloud in savage mockery. Later he will admit his doubts telling Reese, "I trained myself to make things work, not burn 'em up."

A PCA memo on the script of *Hell is for Heroes* objects not only to profanity – the use of "hell" beyond the title – but refers directly to "the scene of the German soldier completely on fire after being hit with a blast from the flame thrower." This it is suggested "would be unacceptably gruesome, and should be suggested rather than shown."[10] It is a sign both of the film's violence and the weakening of the Production Code that the scene appears so directly in the final cut. Reese's violence is also evident in this sequence via his use of a butcher's knife (an association between soldier hero and personalized weaponry that the *Rambo* films will exploit in the 1980s); here the camera occupies the position of a prone German soldier, Reese's knife hacking towards us multiple times. Henshaw's equally grisly death comes via a landmine that wounds him and causes the flamethrower on his back to explode, his screams and dismembered body offering a horrific spectacle. Kolinsky, hit as they retreat screams "my guts, my guts," the camera shooting the scene from above as four men carry the writhing man in his death agonies towards a jeep. These vivid scenes of death in action are a counterpoint to the good war heroism and swift deaths associated with earlier examples of the genre.

Basinger describes *Hell is for Heroes* as not only "one of the great war films," but also as a film that worked against the conventions of the genre, at least those of the period when it was released. What stands out for her is the isolation of the hero as opposed to the group, representing the diversity of the nation operating together, a formation characteristic of the World War II film:

> In its searing finale, Steve McQueen functions as a kind of human war machine, running forward, shooting, throwing packages of explosives into the pillbox under attack. He is shot, falls onto his back into a hole, arms outspread like a Christ figure. But he staggers to his feet, and arises out of the hole like a Frankenstein monster. He falls to his knees again, but repeats his actions, finally throwing himself and the explosives into the pillbox. (2002: 316)

[10] Memo of June 12, 1961, PCA file, Margaret Herrick Library

This "suicide/sacrifice" underlines the fact that death is an immediate and obvious consequence of war, an extension of the logic that has placed the squad in the position they are in, but also a consequence of Reese's warlike character. He is a man fundamentally unsuited to peace.

For Ian Cameron too this "final sequence of the film sums up the whole action, in its picture of the smallness of the contribution an individual can make in an infantry battle" (1973: 96). As Cameron notes the move to a longshot in which men advance and continue to fall suggests the relatively insignificant scale of the gains made, showing the pillbox as one, not particularly significant, feature of the war-blasted landscape. We might contrast this to the shocking death of John Wayne's character in *Sands of Iwo Jima*, juxtaposed as it is with the raising of the flag, with Conway's renewed sense of purpose and patriotic music. The climactic action of *Hell is for Heroes* produces no successor or memorable image.

Director Don Siegel reveals that this bleak ending was not the one originally planned but that he had decided on it during the editing process. He observes:

> The end was more affirmative and we had shot it that way but when I was editing the picture I realized that at the peak of the battle I had nothing else I wanted to say, no feeling of positive affirmation. I wanted to show that my hero was blown up, which was horrifying, and that the rest were still going forward, that he would be forgotten, that the action of the war is futile. I hadn't designed anything for an ending like that, so I optically zoomed in on the pill box. It didn't bother me a bit that it was grainy. It had an authentic quality and it made me feel right about the picture. (Lovell, 1975: 56)

That graininess is of course reminiscent of news footage, the authenticity allied to an aesthetic of documentary realism which, in very different ways, both *Hell is for Heroes* and *Sands of Iwo Jima* exploit.

Although Stuart Kaminsky writes that *Hell is for Heroes* is "clearly an anti-war film" (1974: 198), its stance is not as straightforward as this judgment suggests. As Alan Lovell writes, "In theory it belongs to that genre of anti-war films showing that 'war is hell.' In fact, there is almost no comment on the war itself, which is taken very much for granted" (1975: 71). Indeed Lovell attributes to director Siegel a distinct take on the World War II film's typical characterization of a good war. He writes of Siegel's films more broadly: "the battle between the Americans and the Germans in *Hell is for Heroes* is between two morally or politically undifferentiated groups" (1975: 32). The first assault on the pillbox, led by Reese, fails with him the sole survivor. Asked by Pike, "Were you right?" he responds, blankly staring "How the hell do I know?" Questions of right and wrong seem quaint at best. Moreover, facing a court-martial, and thus exclusion from the combat that gives him purpose, Reese is an embodiment of cynicism and despair as much as heroism and bravery.

Conclusion

The action film begins to emerge as a recognizable genre as the sources upon which it drew, such as the Western and the war movie, themselves evolved. In some part, as detailed in Chapter 1, this is a consequence of the increased prominence of the action sequence. Movies come to feature more action sequences of greater length, a process that clearly impacts on the tone of a film. An increased emphasis on violence and the testing of censorship in relation to its depiction is also a factor, one certainly relevant to the films discussed in this chapter.

In today's sequel oriented Hollywood, killing off the star rarely happens, even in war movies; the death of Miller played by Tom Hanks in *Saving Private Ryan* (1998) is a relatively rare instance. Yet the death of members of the squad, a defining convention of the World War II combat film remains familiar, as is the process of leaning and transformation through combat. Both of the post-war films discussed in this chapter succeed as action films in relatively modern terms, but they also allow and perhaps even require ambivalence about violence and the costs of war.

At a commercial level a clear disadvantage of historically bounded war films is the potential for difficulties in international markets. Republic's decision to distribute a cut version of *Sands of Iwo Jima* in Japan was heavily criticized in a 1952 memo. While the film had initially performed well, it had attracted bad publicity in the Japanese press. Moreover, the film had been cut of unfavorable scenes featuring Japanese soldiers, "therefore reducing the picture's action value tremendously." The anonymous author expresses the view that the release was "in extremely bad taste and definitely against the best interests of the American industry."[11] In subsequent decades American action movies – in particular those involving vast budgets – would come to depend increasingly heavily on international box office and to feature less racially and nationally defined enemies. It is certainly possible to read the aliens of *Battle: Los Angeles* (2011) as analogous to American forces involved in missions overseas (a reading that the film at times seems to invite), yet this remains firmly at the level of the subtext. Nonetheless, the connections between the grizzled Sgt Michael Nantz (Aaron Eckhart) and his squad and the World War II combat film are absolutely clear.

[11] Anonymous memo, 30th July 1952, Margaret Herrick Library

CHAPTER 6

VIOLENCE AND URBAN ACTION: *DIRTY HARRY* (1971)

"*Dirty Harry* ... is the action film's first true archetype"

(Lichtenfeld, 2007: 23)

Throughout the 1960s, Hollywood cinema faced a number of challenges in maintaining and renewing its audience. Tougher – at times even nihilistic – war films such as *The Dirty Dozen* (1967) and *Where Eagles Dare* (1968) were matched by tougher, fast-paced urban crime and vigilante films such as *The French Connection* (1971), with its realist aesthetic and powerful car chase sequence and *Death Wish* (1974), with its brutal staging of urban violence. Historically, crime and gangster films had accelerated those concerns – largely to do with sexual morality – which led to the implementation of the Production Code in Hollywood during the 1930s. The disintegration of the code during the 1960s, and the belated adoption of a ratings system in 1968, mapped a period in which filmmakers pushed the boundaries of acceptability with respect to both sexual and violent imagery. Familiar forms of stylized violence gave way to a grittier, realist aesthetic across

The Hollywood Action and Adventure Film, First Edition. Yvonne Tasker.
© 2015 John Wiley & Sons, Inc. Published 2015 by John Wiley & Sons, Inc.

several action genres. In this context *Dirty Harry* stands for the emergence of a distinctively modern action cinema, synthesizing tropes from earlier action genres, showcasing a tough cop in an unforgiving urban setting, and developing an action aesthetic of gunplay and explosive destruction.

Following the increasingly intense conflict between a San Francisco detective and a deranged sniper/serial killer, Scorpio (Andy Robinson), *Dirty Harry* is perhaps the best known – and widely imitated – of the new kind of urban crime thriller. The sniper targets his victims both at random (the opening shooting, the abduction of a teenage girl) and as representatives of crudely drawn categories co-existing in the city: his ransom notes suggests he will target Catholic priests and black people. Informed by the figure of the Zodiac killer, *Dirty Harry* conveys a sense of the city as a criminal space, a site of danger to all citizens rather than focused on a criminal underworld. Harry's efforts to hunt down Scorpio are consistently thwarted by the city officials, the Mayor's office standing for a corrupt and ineffectual authority superintending a city in which law and order have broken down.

Like *Hell is for Heroes*, discussed in Chapter 5, *Dirty Harry* was directed by Don Siegel. *Hell is for Heroes* had showcased Steve McQueen, one of a new generation of post-war male stars familiar from his television work; McQueen's associations with speed (via his racing) would inform the ground-breaking car chase in his tough cop movie *Bullitt*. In a similar vein, *Dirty Harry* starred Clint Eastwood, an American actor who had initially come to prominence via television and via the Italian Westerns directed by Sergio Leone, and whose association with a tough, modern conservatism were exploited across crime and Western genres in a career spanning decades.[1] Harry

---

[1] As Lichtenfeld notes, *Dirty Harry* was originally to have starred Frank Sinatra who dropped out due to an injury, and to be directed by Irvin Kerschner. A number of high profile male stars, including John Wayne, were offered and rejected the role during the project's development, indicating the controversial character of the material. Each star has distinctly different elements to their persona, with Eastwood bringing associations of both traditionalism and genre revisionism via his Western work. *Dirty Harry* was the fourth film on which Siegel and Eastwood had worked together (2007: 24).

Callaghan proved to be one of Eastwood's most iconic roles with four sequels produced over the coming years (*Magnum Force* [1973], *The Enforcer* [1976], *Sudden Impact* [1983] and *The Dead Pool* [1988]).

Prefiguring what would become familiar concerns over 1980s action cinema, *Dirty Harry* also challenged contemporary reviewers with its attitude to crime and policing. For many critics and commentators the huge popularity of *Dirty Harry* seemed to signal a concerning trend towards cinematic violence and cynicism. Praised for its intensity, the film also sparked contemporary debates around the politics of violence in cinema with some critics regarding the film as an endorsement of vigilantism and of "American fascism." Subsequently, the film has been the subject of a number of studies and has been understood by many as a key film in the development of the contemporary variant of the Hollywood action film. Indeed, as Lichtenfeld summarizes, *Dirty Harry*'s influence "would bring a new mythos to the modern metropolis, and emerge as the prototype for a new, discrete, violent form" (2007: 22). It is, Lichtenfeld argues, the shift from "investigative process" to "the obliteration of criminals" that distinguishes "the police procedural from its successor, the action film" (2007: 4).

Action and the Urban Environment

Dirty Harry begins with a dedication to the San Francisco Police Department, dwelling on the names of those who have died in their duties. Firmly anchored in this way to the authority of the police, the film fades to a foreshortened image of a rifle's barrel against a blue sky; the face of the gunman is obscured though his long hair is evident (despite his targets, the visual association between Scorpio and the cities countercultural youth will be a consistent feature of the film). Next we see through his sights, a young blonde woman in a swimsuit picked out in the crosshairs. As she jumps into the water, the image cuts to a longshot, gradually pulling back to reveal the rooftop pool against the city background. The pool is situated above the city streets and thus seemingly private, but the sniper is higher still. He looks down on the scene from a skyscraper some distance away. The film cuts back to a view of the rifle's barrel, then to the woman leisurely swimming, oblivious to the danger. After a rapid close up of the trigger being depressed, we cut to back to the woman, full screen now, a wound appearing on her back – she turns over, her mouth open in shock, before turning once more to sink beneath the water, her blood spreading through the water.

Dirty Harry paints San Francisco as, if not lawless, then certainly disordered. The random act of violence that initiates the action, directed as it is towards a lone woman within a privileged space of leisure suggests that the city is fundamentally unsafe. Crime pervades the city, exemplified by the sequence in which a robbery intrudes on Harry's meal. The American city as a site of difference and of perversity forms an established theme of the films we now collectively term *film noir*. And for Lichtenfeld, the move made by *Dirty Harry* to couple the themes of the Western – in particular the imposition of law through violence – with the iconography and character types of *noir* is what generates this new urban action mood. Harry Callahan occupies the position of a Western lawman, at odds with both a deranged criminal and with the city authorities, replicating the genre's persistent "triangle composed of the hero, the civilized and the savage" (2007: 24). Yet his violence is transplanted to a different context and transformed in the process, as Lichtenfeld observes: "The most obvious marker of the genre's modernity would be the big-city backdrops that had long served *noir*, detective and gangster picture and against which more classically Western conflicts would now be staged" (2007: 23).

Critics have long drawn a connection between *Dirty Harry's* tough cop and the hard-boiled hero of American crime fiction, more often a private investigator than a member of the official police force. *Noir* cities were frequently scenes of cynical violence as in films such as *Out of the Past* (1947) in which the doomed hero attempts to escape the city, or *Pick Up on South Street* (1953) in which the small time criminal is caught up in an espionage plot. In adaptations of Raymond Chandler's hard-boiled crime novels such as *Murder, My Sweet* (1944), danger awaits the hero at every turn. Action cinema's articulation of urban menace builds on this treacherous – and often somewhat sleazy – *noir* city. For some critics *noir* represented the violence of war brought back home (the figure of the veteran and his potential for violence is a recurrent theme of

American cinema of both the 1940s and the 1970s). Thomas Schtaz writes of hard-boiled films as celebrating,

> ...not the value of law and order or the power of deductive reasoning, but rather the individual style of the isolated hero. This is a man who can deal with the chaos of urban society and still walk away with a shrug. (1981: 136)

Many of *Dirty Harry*'s pursuit scenes are staged at night: Harry and Chico following a suspect down dark alleys; the rooftop stakeout under a revolving neon "Jesus Saves" sign; Harry being run around the city with the ransom money before finally confronting Scorpio in the park, a scene in which Harry is brutally beaten; pursuing Scorpio through the deserted football stadium; tailing him in strip clubs. These night-time scenes use fluid camerawork, coupling an almost documentary sense of the city at night with, if not the stylized qualities of *noir* (its careful compositions and fixed frames), then its equation of dark urban spaces with dubious morality. Not that the film refrains from the symbolism of the city at night: indeed its danger and apparent immorality inform each other, with a persistent religious imagery turning on Harry as a sacrificial figure who is part of yet distanced from the urban context in which he operates.

We can recall here the threat associated with night scenes in the combat movie, discussed in the previous chapter. Those conventions are played out in *Dirty Harry* via a sequence in which Callahan must deliver the ransom money to Scorpio. The latter relishes his power over the policemen, having Callahan race between payphones in different parts of the city. This lengthy game of cat and mouse culminates in a violent confrontation between Harry and Scorpio in the park; here at the foot of a giant cross, Scorpio assaults Callahan who – stripped of his gun – resorts to a hidden flick-knife with which he stabs Scorpio in the leg. No coincidence perhaps that the terrain suggests the field of combat at night – the antagonists emerging from and disappearing into darkness, the sounds of breathing and blows amplified – underlining visual and thematic connections between police and military operations.

While violence frequently takes place within hidden city spaces in *noir*, the Western presents violence out in the open. Most ritualized of all – and most public – is the construction of a small town's main street as a scene of gunplay. The notorious action sequence (discussed later), in which Harry confronts the bank robbers – all young black men – has this quality: brightly lit with city life all around. The floodlit but deserted football stadium in which Harry tortures Scorpio to find the whereabouts of Mary Anne Deakin offers a grotesque inversion of that public performance of justice, the camera pulling away rapidly from the scene of violence. In the Western the location of climatic battles in the center of new communities is a sign of the violence that the establishment of civilization involves. The eradication of criminality is narratively a feature of the past, the formation of America. The restaging of such imagery in urban action films such as *Dirty Harry* is suggestive. However, the final confrontation takes place in location far removed outside the city in a virtually deserted rock quarry, an oddly pastoral site of industry. As Lichtenfeld notes, the quarry, with its rudimentary wooden building, recalls a Western set. The reference is entirely appropriate given that he reads the film as working through Western conventions in a modern setting.

A decade after the film's release Robert Mazzocco wrote in the *New York Review of Books*: "Dirty Harry in the guise of rugged individualist always has to work in a big city where he can be near the action and yet preserve his loner's status." Moreover, he adds, not any city will do since "Such a character can only truly function if set against a presumably 'permissive' milieu like San Francisco." Permissiveness is signaled in ways both socially and morally extensive, the two mapped onto each other from the presence of adult bookstores and theatres, to sexually available women, the city's gay presence and its racial diversity.

Certainly the *noir* city, while often highly stylized and even abstract, perforce gestured towards the racial and ethnic diversity of the urban United States. That representation, as Manthia Diawara points out, was elaborated by African-American writers and filmmakers using themes of race, crime and the city to underscore the divisions of post-war America: "They orient the *noir* style toward a description of a black public sphere and a black way of life" (1993: 263). In urban action films such as *Shaft*, released earlier the same year as *Dirty Harry*, the African American PI hero is supremely powerful and ruthless, a fantasy riposte to the sorts of racial hierarchies played out in Siegel's film in which the alignment of street criminality with black youth affirms and renews urban stereotypes of deviance and subservience. Since American action cinema is propelled by physical action and its conflicts are typically staged in the contemporary, race and power are key themes. The genre has necessarily dealt with – and frequently traded in – the stereotypical racial conventions of Hollywood cinema.

While racial hierarchies underpinned the Western tradition on which it drew, *Dirty Harry* depicts the racial diversity of the city as both more complex and yet equally bound up in images of white authority achieved through violence. The violence of the action city is expressed not only in assaults on the person, but in the very vulnerability of urban spaces to spectacular destruction. Writing of twenty-first century action movies such as *Live Free or Die Hard* and *Transformers* (both 2007), Lisa Purse identifies "urban destruction" as a "fantasy common to the action film" (2011: 66). Clearly such destruction is on a rather more spectacular scale in the *Live Free or Die Hard* set-piece that has Bruce Willis' cop hero John McClane bringing down a helicopter with a car. Yet this impulse to offer a spectacle (whether visual and aural) of the city in chaos is already present in *Dirty Harry*. The film's first – and perhaps most notorious – action sequence establishes the city as a site of destruction as well as danger, even down to the diegetic spectators in the form of construction workers on the nearby scaffolding.

Following a frustrating meeting with the Mayor, Callahan stops for a hot dog; his keen cop eye has already noticed a car idling across the street near a bank. Discerning that a robbery is in progress, he asks the owner to call it in, quietly wishing to himself that events will "just wait until the cavalry arrives." Viewers might wonder whether he really does wish this, given Harry's alignment with violence. In any case the remark seems to trigger the alarm bells across the street and Callahan wanders towards the scene drawing his gun. Still chewing, Harry shouts "Halt" at one of the robbers who emerges from the bank, a command greeted with a rifle shot. Harry shoots the man and as he falls a second robber dives into the car through the window. The car accelerates towards Harry who calmly and deliberately takes aim. Alternating shots contrast the view from the car's interior with images of Callahan whose very immobility signals his power and authority. Editing reinforces Harry's strength in this sequence, cutting on the sound of his shot from Eastwood to the interior of the car and the evident bullet hole in the screen on

PLATE 6.1 The action hero's violence is coupled with an imagery of urban destruction in *Dirty Harry* (1971, directed by Don Siegel and produced by Warner Bros. and The Malpaso Company).

the driver's side. The car turns on its side, demolishing a roadside flower stall and setting off a fire hydrant. The driver is killed and as the passenger flees, firing his weapon, Harry (now represented only by the gun and Eastwood's hands) shoots once more and the man falls dead into the glass of a shop front, his body pictured among the mannequins as civilians scream.

Sound plays an important role in this sequence, mixing together and modulating the sounds of alarms, gunfire, shattering glass, crashing car, gushing water, along with screams, dialogue and the music playing in the getaway car. The violence of the sound is integrated into the city scene. Harry, advancing through the water is a dominating figure and an embodiment of cop violence. In surely the film's most famous moment, Harry taunts the first robber, who is lying wounded but in reach of his rifle, as to whether there any bullets remaining in the weapon Harry is pointing at his head (sneering the much-imitated line, "Do you feel lucky, Punk?"). Here Callahan is playfully sadistic, pre-figuring the final scene in which he will ask the same question of Scorpio even though there can be no doubt of his intentions. In the sequence just described the action underlines Harry's preparedness for violence as well as his superiority defined in racial terms (the opposition to young black criminals who are easily dispatched). While in this city scene Harry's violence is both brutal and yet also official (legitimate, we might say), in the replay at the film's conclusion, his violence is asocial.

Violence against people and property define the action hero. Of course an overturned car that has ploughed into the sidewalk and shattered glass is not on the order of the destruction that comes to the city in, say, *Die Hard* a film that revels in the visceral pleasures of displaying its slick, corporate tower setting progressively shattered, burnt and exploded. Yet the imagery, while on a different scale, is consistent with *Dirty Harry*'s city street; indeed what further connects these movies is an association between the hero and the spectacular destruction of property, civic or corporate. In *Die Hard*, McClane's destructive action brings disapproval, but in *Dirty Harry*, Callahan is praised for his action.

To some extent the action cinema's pleasure in the destruction of property can be seen to target the city as symbolic of the very society that excludes or marginalizes the hero (the Western rarely featured a spectacle of destruction in this way, although the shootout on Main Street is a genre staple). Thus, we see Harry and new partner Chico (Reni Santoni) traverse the city at night, traveling through the streets, illuminated by the storefronts and nightlife that suggest illicit activity. Pursuing a false lead, Harry is taken for a peeping tom, a crowd gathering to dispense rough justice before Chico intervenes. The hero's moral ambivalence is here clearly associated with the city at night.

The Vigilante Hero: Myths of Redemptive Violence

If the opposition of hero and villain is familiar, the intensity of the pursuit and the violence of the conflict between Callahan and Scorpio in *Dirty Harry* suggest a shift in tone within Hollywood cinema from the ritualistic to the sadistic. Comparisons between the two were apparent to several commentators, although few argued that this equivalence was evidence of any ambivalence with respect to the ideological stance of *Dirty Harry*. Significantly perhaps, given subsequent perceptions of the action cinema, the film's ideology was widely discussed. No doubt the negative and eloquent condemnation of the film by the *New Yorker*'s Pauline Kael was a factor. "*Dirty Harry* is obviously just a genre movie," she wrote, "but this action genre has always had a fascist potential, and it has finally surfaced."[2]

[2] Pauline Kael, "Dirty Harry" *New Yorker*, January 15, 1972.

The designation of *Dirty Harry* as a fascist, immoral or irresponsible film was echoed by others. Given the familiarity to contemporary audiences of the conventions in which the film deals, that of the cop who breaks the law to ensure justice for the innocent, it is worth unravelling this claim a little and thinking about its relationship to *Dirty Harry* as an action film – a connection that Kael brings to the fore.

For Kael, the politics are clear and insidious simultaneously. Liberal institutions are posed in *Dirty Harry* as the enemy of good cops doing their job. Miranda and Escobeda rights – directly invoked by a liberal judge – are blamed for the decision to release Scorpio without charge. Having not read Scorpio his rights, but rather tortured him to ascertain the missing teenager's whereabouts, Callahan himself is culpable. Of course, the film presents this state of affairs as absurd, aligning us with the Harry who demands to know who speaks for the murdered girl rather than the Harry who torments the robber in the street or who tortures Scorpio. And since Scorpio is a figure of such abject evil, given no context or background, Harry's tactics seem justified and the liberal politicians who run the city are at best inept. In the context of a figure like Scorpio – "He is pure evil: sniper, rapist, kidnapper, torturer, defiler of all human values" summarizes Kael – such legal rights are simply a charter for criminals to prosper and victims to go unavenged. As Lichtenfeld notes, the film's senior police officers, legal officials and politicians are pictured as "rooted in their offices – their state-sanctioned spaces," whereas Harry is "primarily of the streets" (2007: 24–25). It is he who has the job of enforcing the law, hampered by rules he does not understand ("the law's crazy" he observes in frustration).

The film's ideological framework reflects the concerns of the political right, premised on an assumption that the American justice system accords too many rights to criminals. In the film this leads to Scorpio being freed from custody to commit further crimes. In what is a grotesque scene with distinctly Gothic overtones, Scorpio subsequently pays to be beaten; claiming that Callahan has inflicted the injuries and exploiting the liberal media's concerns, Scorpio is able to ensure that police surveillance (Harry has been following the killer in his own time) is withdrawn. In the film's final sequence, Harry rejects the compromises of his superiors and tackles Scorpio directly. No longer operating officially – the scene is significantly located away from the city – their last encounter results in death rather than capture for Scorpio. In a

PLATE 6.2 Harry Callahan (Clint Eastwood) embodies retributive violence in his climactic confrontation with killer Scorpio. *Dirty Harry* (1971).

gesture towards the bitter ending of the Western *High Noon* (1952), a disaffected Callahan casts his police badge into the water and walks away, the camera pulling back to emphasize his isolation.

In terms of the film's narrative structure, the failing of the legal system effectively defers the confrontation between Callahan and Scorpio until the climactic scene. The result is a distinctive structure whereby the events of the investigation and hunt for Scorpio are doubled, a repetition that allows the stakes to be raised, the violence intensifying towards that climactic confrontation. For Lichtenfeld, "the film's organizing principle is its violent conflicts rather than its ideological ones. The film embodies this in its very structure, with well-regulated intervals between the action sequences that would become the genre's standard" (2007: 28). In retrospect too, it is formally as much as ideologically that *Dirty Harry* has influenced the development of the action film. Its themes of redemptive violence/sacrificial heroism remain of course, but these predate *Dirty Harry* having their cinematic origins in the Western. The film represents an updating and intensification of action filmmaking, characterized by an economical narrative and Eastwood's equally economic performance. The hero is a man of action, showcased within an action narrative; as such no extraneous information that might hamper the development of the narrative is present. That pared down action-oriented structure would become a characteristic of the genre. In *Dirty Harry* it serves to further highlight those ideological themes, expressed through the opposition of hero and villain, which troubled contemporary critics.

Dirty Harry remains perhaps the best known film to articulate a justification for the vigilante hero. In the political context of the late 1960s and early 1970s the film's violent and skillful presentation of these themes proved compelling. If critics agreed on one thing, it was that *Dirty Harry* was an accomplished movie. Indeed to a large extent the ideological critique turned on the view that a film so well made drew audiences expertly into alignment with a dubious position (i.e., that the law should be set aside to achieve justice). Writes Kael, "It would be stupid to deny that *Dirty Harry* is a stunningly well-made genre piece, and it certainly turns an audience on." Deborah Allison cites Kaminsky, noting that even as a consistent champion of Siegel the critic had been forced to conclude that the director "knew what he was doing" and that *Dirty Harry* was "an immoral picture, cracking a revolutionary whip whose sting can only intensify mistrust and suspicion at various levels of society" (2004: n.p.).

Dirty Harry's violence was widely remarked in reviews alongside its politics. The contest between Harry and Scorpio evokes modern forms of deviance and criminality; they wrestle not over land or money (although there is of course a ransom) but over control of the city space and its vulnerable citizens: the victims are all young, exaggeratedly so in the final act in which Scorpio hijacks a school bus and holds the young children on it hostage. In her evaluation of Siegel's work, Allison points to a "refusal to provide an unequivocal demarcation between heroic and villainous activity," with his films often involving an "explicit mirroring between hero and villain" (2004: n.p.). While Eastwood would address the ambivalent aspects of his own cop persona in the later film *Tightrope* (1984), which he also directed, neither film suggests that the questionable character of the police pursuer ultimately overrides the need for a heroic cop figure.

Conclusion: Action Masculinity

In the wake of *Dirty Harry*, action cinema developed the figure of the heroic maverick with enthusiasm. Intuitive rule-breakers who bring destruction in their wake, action heroes are not typically welcomed by figures of authority in movies such as *Die Hard*, a film whose central character bears some debt to Eastwood's Callahan. Like McQueen's Reese in *Hell is For Heroes*, Harry Callahan is a professionally capable figure, a man who gives his all and yet lacks any clear investment in the systems or communities for which he fights. The cowardice of city officials in *Dirty Harry*, their willingness to accede to Scorpio's demands underlines the need for Callahan's violence, just as the death of his wife in a traffic accident points to the losses that seem inherent in urban living. The hero's bewilderment at the District Attorney's refusal to prosecute, judging as he does that Scorpio's rights were violated by Harry's brutal arrest, offers a populist take on contemporary law and order debates. This scenario also forcefully focuses attention on the sort of masculinity the action film requires.

Increasingly with films such as *Dirty Harry* making an impression at the box office, scholarship has explored the values associated with the figure of the white male hero and the sorts of stars who have played this role. Clint Eastwood's transition from Western hero to hard-boiled cop seems to be an indicative trajectory in terms of the genre more broadly, not that he abandoned Western roles entirely – he would gain Academy Award as Best Director for his 1992 *Unforgiven*. These strong associations with the genre in turn inform *Dirty Harry* with its contradictory coupling of frontier justice and the modern city. The Eastwood star persona develops in line with the emergence of an American action cinema in the 1960s, 1970s and 1980s.

To some extent of course the generic juxtaposition (Western and urban cop film) works to underline Harry Callahan's position as a hero who does not quite fit; his resistance to the rules of the City, his tendency to lose his police partners to violence and his racism – whether it is actually felt or humorously performed – suggests that Callahan does not comfortably inhabit modern American urban life. Indeed Susan Jeffords writes that "Harry's heroism has a nihilistic edge to it that cannot reassure audiences that any of his actions have mattered or have changed the social order in any way" (1993: 19). While he dispatches Scorpio outside the city, and thus saves the children in the school bus the killer has hijacked, the ending is downbeat. Moreover, the parallels between licit and illicit violence are themselves a component of the film.

Lovell remarks: "If Siegel is ever remembered as being more than an action director, he is remembered as a director whose films are marked by excessive violence" (1975: 25). For Lovell this is a misguided view, since he argues that violence is not excessive but rather targeted and coupled to the themes of Siegel's films. What seems clear, however, is that the sort of violent masculinity that functions to redeem a corrupt society and that is embodied in the hero would come to dominate American action cinema.

In his retrospective overview of *Dirty Harry*, Rick Thompson writes that "stylistically, the film looks and sounds remarkably contemporary" (2000: n.p.). In part that contemporary feel stems from the widespread influence of the film within the emergent action cinema. That influence is evidence in rogue cop heroes such as Martin Riggs in the *Lethal Weapon* films and John McClane in the *Die Hard* series. These films are perhaps more spectacular and, if possible, fantastical in the scope of the criminality the heroes confront. They also insist on developing bi-racial partnerships as central components of the fictional world. And yet the conventions and characterization, the glee in disregarding rules and regulations and the spectacular destruction of property, suggests a through-line of development for the American action hero.

CHAPTER 7

NOSTALGIC ADVENTURE AND RECYCLED CULTURE: *RAIDERS OF THE LOST ARK* (1981) AND *PIRATES OF THE CARIBBEAN* (2003)

Vera Dika remarks that "the impulse to copy old images and old films is itself moving into its second generation" (2003:1), citing *Raiders of the Lost Ark* as one of this trend's "first sightings," along with movies such as *Star Wars* (directed by George Lucas, the producer of *Raiders*). *Raiders* effectively reworked the serial and fantasy adventures of an earlier era, employing spectacular effects to update the appearance of the adventure film. Perhaps because of this blockbuster B movie quality, the film is also cited by Fredric Jameson in his influential discussions of postmodern cinema as a reworking of past conventions divorced from history. Art historian Noël Carroll also mentions *Raiders* in his discussion of allusion as an aesthetic strategy in the Hollywood cinema of the 1970s.

Pirates of the Caribbean (2003) based on a Disney theme park attraction, surely exemplifies the second generation of reworking to

---

The Hollywood Action and Adventure Film, First Edition. Yvonne Tasker.
© 2015 John Wiley & Sons, Inc. Published 2015 by John Wiley & Sons, Inc.

which Dika refers. *Pirates* has not attracted the interest of art historians or cultural theorists in the way that *Raiders* did. No less commercially successfully and culturally visible, the difference is surely that what struck many as new when *Raiders* appeared – the large-screen, spectacular reworking of largely forgotten or low status source materials – was a familiar strategy by the time that *Pirates of the Caribbean* voyaged to the multiplexes.

While the effects in *Pirates of the Caribbean* are very much a product of digital technologies and *Raiders of the Lost Ark* used locations and stunt work, there are some aesthetic commonalities: both films couple adventure narratives, inventive action sequences, spectacular (at times gruesome) effects and humor. They underline the continued pertinence of adventure cinema as a reference point for analyses of action; indeed thinking about the work of adventure space and adventure time in these movies underscores the usefulness of these concepts for analyzing even those action movies set in the "here and now." In common with a number of other franchises – such as those based around the *Lord of the Rings* and *Harry Potter* books – *Raiders of the Lost Ark* and *Pirates of the Caribbean* are themselves perpetuated and renewed through sequels, merchandising, console and other games, rides and, of course, imitators. In total these franchises mobilize an extraordinarily high degree of cultural visibility. As such, alongside the interest that the Indiana Jones films have held for scholars interested in the postmodern repetition of past cultural forms, they are also very much part of contemporary commercial Hollywood. Indeed, there is no contradiction between the two perspectives: allusion may be a feature of postmodern style, but recycled culture is a staple of commerce.

Produced 30 years after *Raiders*, *Pirates of the Caribbean* exemplifies action and adventure cinema's continued investment in recycled culture, specifically pirate adventure that had long fallen out of favor. Successful sequels appeared in 2006, 2007 and 2011, developing *Pirates of the Caribbean* into a franchise (a fifth film is in development). The use of period settings can be thought of in terms of a sort of "heritage action," albeit of a rather different kind to the period piece played out in *Crouching Tiger, Hidden Dragon* (see Chapter 8). Neither is this the sort of historical adventure with which Taves is concerned, the supernatural elements of the film suggesting a broader generic basis. Indeed, both *Pirates of the Caribbean* and *Raiders of the Lost Ark* draw our attention not just to the theme of recycled culture or to the rich diversity of action and adventure in Hollywood's past, but also to the generic hybridity– the merging of different generic elements, sometimes producing surprising juxtapositions – of its present form.

Raiders of the Lost Ark: Adventure Cinema and Historical Pastiche

An archaeologist adventurer hero, a college professor more at ease in the field, Indiana Jones combines in one figure the characteristics that are frequently divided across two characters in adventure films and serials: the impulsive, young and physically active hero and the smart older advisor. Jones is both intuitive and brave, his deficiencies being in the realm of emotion and morality rather than intellect or integrity. Cast as a solo figure, Jones typically acquires a companion in the films, albeit one who requires his protection. Jones' adventures are played out first in *Raiders of the Lost Ark* and subsequently in three other films: *Indiana Jones and the Temple of Doom* (1984), *Indiana Jones and the Last Crusade* (1989) and *Indiana Jones and the Kingdom of the Crystal Skull* (2008). These movies operate in an *adventure space* of international travel, danger and opportunity, and in an *adventure time* that is comfortably in the past albeit a time of considerable turmoil in the run-up to World War II (the exception is *Crystal Skull*, produced almost 20 years later and set in 1957 to take account of lead actor Harrison Ford's ageing).

Indiana Jones is a hero styled to act in both adventure space and adventure time (the improbable ocean voyage with Indie *outside* a German submarine). Adventure time allows the imagining of the past as a site of relative freedom for the American hero who roams the world seeking its treasures – all to be placed in American museums for their safekeeping. Of course time is in some ways quite specific in *Raiders*, linked as it is to the pre-war years. And yet the Nazis who are searching for an ancient relic, the Ark of the Covenant, act as stereotypical villains familiar from countless war movies. Indeed the film's chief villain is not a Nazi but another archaeologist/mercenary, Belloq (Paul Freeman), whose similarity to Jones makes for a more interesting antagonism than that with the comic book German villains or their Egyptian henchmen. The opposition between Belloq and Jones is introduced early in *Raiders*; once Jones has successfully managed to purloin the golden idol in the opening sequence, Belloq takes it from him, backed up by a native tribe. In adventure movie tradition, these native warriors are wordless, menacing and yet somehow unable to assail the hero – Jones escapes a large number of pursuers (armed with bows and arrows and poisoned darts) without a scratch. That comic play of indestructible western hero and his/her antagonist underpins a well-known image from the film in which Jones, disheveled from fighting off a number of anonymous and seemingly disposable Egyptian heavies, confronts a more physically imposing fighter equipped with a sword, shrugs and shoots him thereby undercutting the elaborate display of swordsmanship. The moment is played as comedy both because it undercuts the expectations of a prolonged action/combat sequence but also because of its exploitation of racial stereotypes and hierarchies.

Discussion of racial hierarchies and of racism in the Indiana Jones films has understandably focused on *Indiana Jones and the Temple of Doom*, which attracted some notoriety for its portrayal of a blood-thirsty Kali-worshipping Thugee sect. With its banquet of monkey brains, scenario of child slavery and grotesque imagery of human sacrifice, *Temple of Doom* presents India as a site of horror and oppression, a depiction that caused considerable offence for its inaccuracy over Indian religion and culture (the film's violence was also a source of concern in popular commentaries). Jones is a cynical savior against this landscape, once again interested only in the prize. If *Temple of Doom* was intense enough to cause comment, the treatment of native peoples as a backdrop to the concerns of the western protagonists, the use of racial stereotypes and the casting of western actors in significant roles (British actors John Rhys-Davis as Sallah and Alfred Molina as the treacherous assistant in the opening sequence) is familiar territory.

Both the enormous commercial success of *Raiders of the Lost Ark* and its evident cinephilic nostalgia – that is, its immersion in American film history – attracted commentary at the time and in the years following its release. To some extent *Raiders* came to stand for wider trends in the industry such as the emergence of the summer block-buster, and the importance in advertising of an ability to condense a film into a promotional image (Indiana Jones' distinctive costume of leather jacket, whip and fedora). Noël Carroll describes *Raiders* as a work of "historical pastiche," situating the film within a broader context within which "allusion, specifically to film history, has become a major expressive device" (1982: 51–52). Like other critics, Carroll identifies the slightly uncanny quality that stems from the film's highly accomplished rendition of its low budget sources; following the revisionism of previous decades wherein films had revisited the conventions of the cinematic past in order to critique them (notably in the Western), *Raiders'* aesthetic nostalgia was indeed rather striking.

Raiders signals the vigor and the potential of action-adventure franchises built around strong, iconic characters. Although routinely described as pastiche, *Raiders* is characterized by not only a sincere affection for the film traditions it reworks (though the film exploits comedy, it is not a parody), but strong performances across leading and supporting roles, accomplished action sequences and a script that developed the narrative with humor and economy. While Spielberg apparently had in mind an ambition to make a film similar to the Bond movies, with international settings and action set-pieces, *Raiders* adopts a very different stance towards its globetrotting hero. Larry Gross observes of the comparison: "George Lucas said that he conceived of Indiana Jones in exact opposition to James Bond, as a hero with a whip and a hat rather than machinery" (2000: 9). Thus, although Jones conspicuously adds a pistol to his suitcase to supplement the whip, observing that he is a "cautious fellow," he is certainly a low-tech hero in comparison to Bond. The action sequences in *Raiders or the Lost Ark* are always spectacular, however. Moreover, they keep Jones firmly in view, an urgently mobile and driven figure on whom the action centers.

Gross entertainingly and not inaccurately describes the narrative structure of *Star Wars* as "A chase, a chase, a chase and a chase." He adds:

By the time they made *Raiders* together, the two [Spielberg and Lucas] had the chase structure down to such precise levels of control that they got ten or 12 into the film (with sub-chases in some chases). The concept of the Ride is now fully in place. (2000: 8)

Raiders of the Lost Ark is certainly structured around its action set-pieces, from the opening foray in South America to recover a sacred golden figure – a quest that culminates in the hero being chased by a vast boulder – through to the climatic spectacle sequence in which the Ark is opened by, and brings destruction to, Belloq and the Nazis who employ him. And yet it seems somewhat blithe to assert that the number and regularity of action sequences involves, as Gross suggests, an "ability to make the visual sensation answer all questions of meaning and value" (2000: 8). Such comments return to the often expressed view that action sequences (and by extension action cinema) involve spectacles devoid of content; that these set-piece sequences, while technically accomplished, do nothing to advance a film's narrative or to add to its thematic complexity, in short that they lack meaning or value. In such a view, action, and the thrills that it offers, tends towards the reduction or even the eradication of psychological complexity.

How might the action sequences in *Raiders of the Lost Ark* be considered other than in technical terms? The image of Indiana Jones running towards the screen, boulder behind him, is now iconic and the contrast between this first set-piece and the climactic scene of supernatural violence on the unnamed island is marked: in the first Jones is the active figure, "raiding" a temple for the golden idol and outwitting the traps set for such opportunist thieves, while in the second he is tied to a stake – a passive onlooker, indeed not even that since he and Marian (Karen Allen) shut their eyes and thus avoid destruction. Reading the trilogy through the frame of Arthurian romance, Susan Aronstein points to the process of transformation that Indiana Jones undergoes through the course of the film. She details "Indiana's conversion to the proper moral authority as he learns to take responsibility for the 'objects' of his quest" (1995: 3). For Aronstein that shift or conversion turns on Jones' relationship to Marian (of which more later). It is expressed visually and narratively, however, through the two action sequences mentioned previously that spectacularly establish Jones first as daring thief and ultimately as a hero who knows when to step/look away. In the process of course the film underlines that America really is the safest place for such powerful weapons as the Ark, dovetailing with an argument that the commercial cinema of the 1980s was ultimately conservative. Aronstein too holds this view, although she considerably complicates it, arguing that the first two Indiana Jones films, in their portrayal of an American hero who assumes the world is his to collect and yet ultimately acts responsibly, operate to "both condemn and redeem the mistakes of pre-Reagan America" (1995: 16).

Before turning to Marian's role, it is worth considering *Raiders'* action sequences in more detail. While the climactic scene features a physically constrained hero and stages a range of special effects to achieve its supernatural destruction (not least the melting face of Toht, the villainous SS officer), this is not typical of the perils faced by the hero. Indeed, of the seven principle action sequences, it is only the last – in which the participants are destroyed – that does not have Jones as the focus. The contest for ownership of the Ark, once Jones and Sallah have discovered it, involves three linked thrilling action sequences: the escape from the Well of Souls (incorporating snakes and skeletons), the one-on-one fight at the airstrip (preventing the Ark from being transported by air) with the extended chase on horseback and then in, on and under a German truck that wins the Ark for Indiana Jones. With Jones pursuing the German convoy on horseback, *Raiders* evokes the Western, and thus, America; in his subsequent commandeering, loss and recapture of the truck containing the Ark, Jones is both intrepid and relentless. Throughout the chase the hero's dynamism, persistence and bravery are celebrated. The desert setting offers an abstracted adventure space for conflict. Towards the end of the

PLATE 7.1 Mobilizing the iconography of the Western adventure hero: Indiana Jones (Harrison Ford) in *Raiders of the Lost Ark* (1981, directed by Steven Spielberg and produced by Paramount Pictures and Lucasfilm).

chase, the setting moves from the uninhabited space of the desert to a recognizable and populated Egypt; the irrigation systems that the truck smashes into suggests the destruction associated with both Indie and his antagonists, while at the culmination of the chase the truck, now in Indie's possession, is hidden by the townspeople suggesting their resistance to the German forces.

The flames and explosions that end several of the action sequences – the fight in the bar, the chase through the marketplace and the fight at the airstrip – all call up the iconography of a World War II film. The explosion is now a fixed component of action cinema of course, part of an aesthetic of destruction touched on at different points in this book but in the cinema of the 1930s and 1940s to which *Raiders* refers, it was most often a war movie convention. The spectacular explosion that closes *White Heat* (1949), for example, underlines that film's status as a larger scale, post-war recycling of the earlier gangster movie cycle. Each explosion in *Raiders* marks a narrative ending in visually dramatic form: the destruction of Marian's bar that leads to her insistence on accompanying Jones; the explosion of the jeep in the marketplace that the audience and Jones believes has killed Marian; the explosion of the plane that allows a chase over land.

Marian is an important symbolic figure in these sequences. We've seen that female action heroes became more prominent – although hardly commonplace – in the genre during the 1980s, and that the narrative of *Raiders* turns on Jones relationship to Marian. Adventure cinema, with its past settings and nostalgic tendencies, typically retains the narrative function accorded to woman as prize. In *Raiders of the Lost Ark* Marian Ravenswood is as much beyond the boundaries of conventions of behavior as Indiana Jones himself, more so perhaps given the codes of femininity that operated in 1980s cinema. She is introduced winning a drinking contest in the bar she owns and runs in Nepal. On Indiana's arrival (he is introduced as a menacing shadow on the wall), she rebukes him for his behavior years before, a story of seduction and betrayal that put a rift between Jones and his former teacher/mentor, Marian's father. Once the romantic/sexual object of Jones' interest, Marian is now desirable for what she possesses, a medallion collected by her father that reveals the location of the lost Ark.

Many of the film's action sequences involve Indiana and Marian together from the brawl in her bar, the chase through the market and the fight at the airstrip. Yet her role in the action is strictly limited and frequently comic. In the chase through the market, for instance, she employs a frying pan to disarm one pursuer before hiding in a basket and being literally carried away. During the airstrip fight Marian is trapped in the plane; this enables her to use the mounted machine gun to kill advancing German soldiers, but containers of fuel are also hit, creating a trail of fire so that she must be rescued moments before the plane itself explodes. Marian's violence is thus uncontrolled and almost inadvertent. Ultimately then *Raiders* maintains a gendered hierarchy that reserves heroism for men.

Pirates of the Caribbean: Theme Park Cinema

If it is by now a commonplace to cite the analogy between action and adventure films and the ride – thrills, visceral effects and sweeping camerawork suggesting or simulating a rollercoaster experience – *Pirates of the Caribbean* (2003), based on a Disney theme park attraction seemed to literalize the connection. The film contains all the pirate adventure tropes one might expect: swordplay, fighting across the rigging and swinging from ropes, falling from heights, diving into the sea and walking the plank. In one scene a screaming Elizabeth Swann (Keira Knightley) is tossed into the air by undead pirates: a ride of sorts. Her screaming face races up to the camera, before a skeleton crew member swings in on a rope to whisk her away, pursuing her around the deck. Yet as discussed in Chapter 3, the analogy of movie as ride masks as much as it reveals. The Disney theme parks encompass both rollercoaster, speed-oriented rides and evocative, spectacle-based but also strongly theme and narrative driven rides such as *Pirates of the Caribbean* – itself a nostalgic trip through pirate adventure conventions (in reference to one of the ride's tableaux, Jack Sparrow tells prisoners in the cell next to him who are attempting to lure the jailor's dog, keys clutched in its mouth, that, do what they will "the dog is *never* going to move"). And as Geoff King writes: "Often driven by the demand to produce immersive and/or interactive spectacle, film-based rides and computer games maintain a significant investment in narrative, as do the films on which they draw" (2000: 189).

In 2006 the "Pirates of the Caribbean" ride was modified to include elements from the films including the figure of Jack Sparrow who appears at different points along the journey, replete with quirky gestures. In 1989 Disney had opened an attraction based on the Indiana Jones films at its Hollywood Studios Park in Florida. The "Indiana Jones Epic Stunt Spectacular!" show is organized around the theme of special effects, purporting to let audiences in on some of the magic of the movies via the work of stunt performers, on-set explosions and the camera crew. Movie-making itself serves as an attraction (including the explosions that are so strongly associated with adventure cinema), just as these films acknowledge their pleasure in film history. The experiential qualities of action and adventure are thus incorporated into the theme park spectacle.

The theme park origins of *Pirates of the Caribbean*, that is, do not in themselves mean a spectacle stripped of narrative interest. The film's narrative is structured around the intense desires of its lead characters: Captain Jack Sparrow's (Johnny Depp) desire to recover his ship, the *Black Pearl*, wrested from him by his mutinous crew before the film begins; the frustrated romance between Elizabeth Swann and blacksmith Will Turner (Orlando Bloom); the quest of Sparrow's former First Mate, Captain Barbossa (Geoffrey Rush) and his pirate crew to escape the curse of the Aztec gold that holds them unable to enjoy life or to die. Each of these plot lines are interconnected, with the characters desires conflicting: Barbossa has the *Black Pearl* but requires Will Turner's blood to lift the curse; Will loves Elizabeth who is kidnapped by Barbossa – he needs Jack's help to find her; Jack wants the *Black Pearl* back but to take it most defeat an undead opponent.

Pirates of the Caribbean reputedly took some years to come to fruition, largely since it was felt that pirate films were not a safe commercial prospect.[1] The success of *Pirates of the Caribbean* is in this sense intriguing as an example of recycled culture: no pirate film had performed well for years, the ride itself dated to the 1960s and was steeped

---

[1] The financially ruinous Geena Davis vehicle *Cutthroat Island* (1995) no doubt underlined the point. Nonetheless, if the pirate movie has not fared well in New Hollywood, other swashbuckling traditions had been effectively rebooted – as in the various versions of Zorro, Musketeers and Robin Hood tales.

in the genre imagery of the 1950s, and star Johnny Depp was not associated (at that time) with big blockbuster projects. Indeed *Pirates of the Caribbean* exemplifies twenty-first century adventure cinema not in its use of a moribund sub-genre but in its commercially smart recycling of familiar cultural forms to appeal to new audiences.

In line with the Hollywood adventure tradition, *Pirates of the Caribbean* equates piracy with freedom. That is how Jack, drunk with rum, describes the *Black Pearl* to Elizabeth, as "freedom": "Wherever we want to go, we go – that's what a ship is." In some classical pirate films this freedom is literal. Thus, in *Captain Blood* (1935), Errol Flynn's Peter Blood is a surgeon unjustly enslaved for treating a rebel. He escapes the brutality of slavery for a life of piracy and revenge. A good man, Blood is clearly opposed to the film's amoral pirate Levasseur (Basil Rathbone), who symbolizes freedom rather too aggressively it seems. Pirate films typically showcase a less noble heroism as Taves writes: "Relishing their unrespectable status, pirates range from disgruntled nonconformists to antisocial dropouts and undesirables who find themselves unable to live by ordinary laws or means" (1993: 28). The freedom of the pirate is then, more or less explicitly, a rejection of society.

During the 1950s Hollywood pirate films had become increasingly stylized, at times camp. *The Crimson Pirate* (1958), an accomplished genre piece, opened with a grinning Burt Lancaster amidst the rigging, directing the crew below before turning to the camera and addressing the audience directly; Lancaster describes the tale as taking place "a long, long time ago in the far, far Caribbean" challenging viewers to believe only "half of what you see," advice that follows a spectacular image of the bare-chested star swinging via a rope from one mast to another. One-time acrobat Lancaster's athleticism in the role emphasizes the choreographed quality of the action. The action is organized around a narrative of rebellion, yet the film's tone is less to do with freedom than with humor, coupling hearty masculine heroics with a camp enthusiasm for pirate clichés.

In *Pirates of the Caribbean* the undead pirate crew besieges Port Royal, invading its homes and bringing destruction; they are abject figures, grotesque and darkly comic. The film makes a running joke of its references to the Pirate Code, to rights of parlay and other conventions familiar to viewers through childhood texts (for decades pirates have featured within children's rather than adult film culture). And it is clear that characters who are not pirates themselves, notably Elizabeth and Will, are more than familiar with – and even entranced by – popular stories and myths. The pirate code, earnestly recounted by Flynn in the definitive pirate film of the classical era, *Captain Blood*, becomes a pre-text for humor and treachery in *Pirates of the Caribbean*. When Elizabeth insists that the code be respected, Captain Barbossa (Geoffrey Rush) responds that it consists of "more what you call guidelines than actual rules." A similar error of judgment catches out Will Turner during a spirited and inventive duel with Jack Sparrow that takes place in the smithy. When the latter throws dust in his face and draws a pistol, Will protests "you cheated" to which Jack, by way of wry comment, replies "pirate." In modern action films, heroes are enterprising in precisely this way; Will's adherence to the rules of sword fighting suggest how straitlaced he is, quite as much as the inability to confess his feelings to Elizabeth evident in the film's early scenes. Will's naive adherence to codes of honor provide a humorous contrast to Jack's schemes.

In narrative terms *Pirates of the Caribbean* is structured as Elizabeth's story. The film's opening scene depicts her aboard ship as a young girl longing for the romance of pirate adventure. Amongst the mist she spots the body of a boy, Will Turner, floating on an improvised raft, discovering a medallion around his neck that suggests he is a pirate. Elizabeth wakes as a young woman, suggesting that the previous scenes were a dream yet she proceeds to take the medallion from a dusty hiding place; her honesty shortly after when she sees Turner, now a blacksmith's apprentice, in telling him that she had dreamt of him the night before confirms her distance from the stuffy formality and constraints of the day. Such formality and its physical and metaphorical discomfort for women is figured in the form of a corseted dress that Elizabeth's father gives her as a gift. It is this constraining dress – which comically prevents her from breathing properly – that results in her fainting and falling from the castle walls into the sea in the early part of the film. In turn, this triggers the story proper since the medallion's contact with the water seems to call up the *Black Pearl* with its ghostly crew.

Like Rose in *Titanic*, or Evelyn (Rachel Weisz) in *The Mummy* (1999), these opening scenes set Elizabeth up as an independent heroine frustrated by, and to some extent at odds with, the conventions of the day. Uninspired by the prospect of a "smart match" with Commodore Norrington (Jack Davenport), Elizabeth is drawn instead to Will Turner. Through the course of the film she will shift further into the position of adventurer, signaled in part by costume. Held by the undead pirates she is forced to wear a fine gown, functioning as object of display; much later she will borrow soldier's clothes, setting to work to rescue Will. This cross-dressing underlines her departure from conventional femininity, a process that begins when Jack Sparrow cuts the constricting corset away. Indeed pitching into the film's climactic battle she proclaims "You like pain? Try wearing a corset!" As Antje Ascheid writes (2006), despite the action context, this image sits comfortably within a female-focused heritage film trend that portrays a "proto-feminist fantasy" of liberation. Thus, if piracy signals the freedom to travel for Jack, *Pirates of the Caribbean* constructs a strong female lead for whom freedom resonates in terms of gender conventions.

Martin Fradley explores the ideological work of *Pirates of the Caribbean*, a film series he notes is too often dismissed as obvious. He sees its depiction of "pirate society as a liminal fantasy space of gender adventurism and wilful sexual indeterminacy" (2012: 300), with Elizabeth conforming to O'Day's formulation of "action babe cinema." By the end of the third film she has transformed, Fradley suggests, "from colonial subject to swashbuckling pirate" (2012: 309) a transformation emblematic of the series' investment in feminine power and the transgression of rules. *Pirates* stages a relatively genteel rebellion against a corseted past. Nonetheless, we might contrast this to Karen Allen's role as the female lead in *Raiders of the Lost Ark*. Despite her obvious adventurous spirit, her sphere of action is limited, in narrative terms being primarily confined to serving as contested object between Indiana Jones and Belloq. In the second film (a prequel, set the previous year) *Indiana Jones and the Temple of Doom*, the love interest role is taken by the increasingly hysterical Willie, the sidekick function performed instead by a child, Short Round. The third film's sparring is between Jones and his father while the fourth – produced much later – reunites Indiana with the female lead of the original film. All of this suggests that female characters with agency were something of a problem for the Indiana Jones series. In the two decades between *Raiders of the Lost Ark* and *Pirates of the Caribbean* – both films that use past settings for their combination of action and romance – some notable shifts have taken place in the presence and function of women in action and adventure. The mainstreaming of the action heroine is one notable feature, although there remain clear limits around women's activity in many action and adventure films.

As played by Johnny Depp, Captain Jack Sparrow is a charismatic creation though no obvious adventure hero. He is also something of a preposterous figure, a "popinjay pirate" remarks David Denby, delivered by Depp in a "fey, capering performance" (2003: n.p.). A pirate without a ship or crew, Sparrow's authority is continually undercut even while his (quirky) hero status is affirmed. Consider his first appearance: the camera sweeps up towards Sparrow stood atop a mast, his back towards us, long hair caught like the flag beside him in the wind. Sparrow surveys the scene from a position of mastery, seemingly intent on a ship anchored near a headland in the middle distance. Cut to a reverse angle, again moving upwards, the camera closes in on Sparrow's face as the distinctive pirate theme is heard on the sound track. This is the romantic image of the pirate, his face expressionless and his figure set against a brooding, stormy sky. He glances down, grabs a rope and leaps – only to land in the water that is filling the craft. Another cut reveals the vessel as nothing more than a small boat, and a sinking one at that. The mastery of the opening shots is undercut with physical comedy that sketches the hero's dilemma.

PLATE 7.2 *Pirates of the Caribbean* evokes and affectionately mocks the romantic image of the pirate: Johnny Depp as Captain Jack Sparrow (2003, directed by Gore Verbinski and produced by Walt Disney Pictures and Jerry Bruckheimer Films).

A further series of shots give Sparrow's point of view on three skeletons, bodies left hanging as a warning – they are juxtaposed with a
crude wooden sign "Pirates, Ye be Warned" and a spare noose. Doffing
his hat and saluting these long-dead corpses, Sparrow's eccentricity is
confirmed. Nonetheless, he is able to make an almost elegant entrance
to Port Royal; his boat sinks as it approaches the dock, allowing him
to step neatly off. This entrance is followed by a scene of verbal banter
with two British soldiers, firmly establishing Sparrow's eccentricity
and trickster status. Shortly after he dives into the sea to rescue
Elizabeth, thus demonstrating bravery appropriate to the action-
adventure hero. Apprehended, he is described by Norrington as
"without doubt, the worst pirate I've ever heard of." Jack's vanity and
concern for his reputation is evident in the retort "But you *have* heard
of me." Using Elizabeth as a shield to escape, Jack's daring pirate
character is once more restored as he leaps and slides to safety.

These abrupt reversals – figure of fun, heroic action figure –
encapsulate the dual role played by Captain Jack Sparrow in the film.
Just as in *The Adventures of Robin Hood*, discussed in Chapter 4, the
vitality of the outlaw figures is signaled by their freedom of movement
set against the ranks of Normans, here the pirate adventurer is contrasted to the regimented formality of the colonial military. Jack
Sparrow's peculiar mannerisms – adopting the pose of an adventurer
though not quite pulling it off – draw out the comic qualities of the
material, even while we are asked to accept him as a credible leader.
Writes Fradley, "Although Sparrow occasionally performs in the traditional heroic mode, generally his swashbuckling escapades are more
ambiguously coded" (2012: 303). As with the character of Indiana
Jones, Jack Sparrow's hat and costume define his character, iconic in
their recognizability (and marketability).

"Even when cast in the heroic mold," writes Taves, "pirates are not
as clean living, patriotic, or moral as most other adventurers" (1993: 27).
Pirates of the Caribbean successfully acknowledges, exploits and (cru-
cially) decouples from the romance plot, both the immorality and the
camp aspects of the Hollywood pirate movie, a quality that by the
early 2000s seemed immovable. Johnny Depp's humorous posturing
and distinctive look in the role is contrasted to the conventionally
styled romantic hero, Will Turner. Orlando Bloom was clearly associated with fantasy adventure via his role as Legolas in the *Lord of the*

Rings movies. That Turner is ultimately revealed to be the son of a pirate and a fine swordsman, also renders him romantic enough for the film's sole significant female character, Elizabeth Swann.

The film's tagline – "Prepare to be blown out of the water" – promised spectacle and, implicitly, innovation on the basic elements familiar from the genre and indeed the ride itself. *Pirates* effectively took the ghostly overtones of the ride (the skeletons in the opening section) along with the scenes of comic destruction of Tortuga, coupling these with Hollywood's swashbuckling adventure tradition and horror movie imagery. Like the successful series of *Mummy* films (1999, 2001, 2008), *Pirates of the Caribbean* couples action and romance with digital effects evoking bodily instability and decay. In *The Mummy* Imhotep's body collapses, decays and reforms through the course of the film while scarab beetles burrow under the skin of luckless victims. Adventurer Rick (Brendan Fraser) and Egyptologist Evelyn (Rachel Weisz) fall in love as they battle the ancient forces.

Pirates of the Caribbean pits its heroes against a supernatural foe in the form of Barbossa's cursed pirates; that supernatural element would become a recurrent feature of the sequels. While *The Mummy* used effects to showcase the creature at the film's center and the powers he commands, *Pirates* visual effects center on the revelation of an undead pirate crew whose true form is only seen in moonlight. These monstrous figures are both grotesque and comic, as with the running gag of one character popping his artificial eye in and out, mislaying it and rediscovering it. The swordplay sequences recall Harryhausen's stop-motion skeletons but the emphasis on adventure means that horror is played down. And in line with adventure conventions over those of horror, ultimately each of the major characters will get what they want: the curse is lifted, Will and Elizabeth are united, Jack regains the *Black Pearl*. Jack also has the last word, a final pirate cliché – "drink up me hearties – yo ho!" – which underlines the film's character as both affectionate pastiche and full-blown action film.

CHAPTER 8

ACTION BLOCKBUSTERS IN THE 1980S: *RAMBO: FIRST BLOOD PART II* (1985) AND *DIE HARD* (1988)

"*Rambo* seems to be on everyone's mind these days."

Andrew Sarris (1985: 53)

Action and adventure cinema became increasingly prominent commercially during the 1980s. One distinctive strand of that blockbuster cinema was the historical adventure spectacle exemplified by *Raiders of the Lost Ark*. Such films were light-hearted in tone, spectacular in form and typically targeted family audiences. A second strand, which has attracted rather more critical comment to date, is exemplified by major commercial successes such as the *Lethal Weapon* (1987, 1989, 1992, 1998), *Beverley Hills Cop* (1984, 1987, 1994), *Die Hard* (1988, 1990, 1995, 2007, 2013) and *Rambo* (1982, 1985, 1998, 2008) films. Firmly contemporary in setting, though arguably no less fantastic in character (explicitly so in the case of *The Terminator* and its sequels), these films developed and reinvigorated existing action and adventure tropes, honing what are now familiar action formulae: the

The Hollywood Action and Adventure Film, First Edition. Yvonne Tasker.
© 2015 John Wiley & Sons, Inc. Published 2015 by John Wiley & Sons, Inc.

destruction of property; images of the tortured/damaged hero and comic banter between antagonistic partners.

Driven in part by an emerging video rental market – which required new designations, if nothing else than to mark out the shelves in stores – these titles brought action cinema as a generic descriptor into clearer view. Now a staple of film reviewing and advertising practice, it was during the 1980s that a distinct action movie – as against the action genres of previous decades such as the Westerns, gangster film or crime thriller – came into view. The genre was evidently directed towards young adult filmgoers, featuring more vivid depictions of violence than had been the norm in adventure films and language that (as much as the violence) generated restrictive certificates. The revived action cinema of the 1980s forged new stars, among them Arnold Schwarzenegger, Bruce Willis, Eddie Murphy and Sylvester Stallone. That Murphy, and to some extent Willis, were performers associated primarily with comedy is telling; the combination of action and comedy would become familiar, exploited in commercial successes such as *Rush Hour* (1998).

This chapter centers on a discussion of two films that proved to be huge commercial successes in the 1980s: *Rambo: First Blood Part II* and *Die Hard*. Each generated sequels extending into the twenty-first century. The most recent *Rambo* (2008) and *A Good Day to Die Hard* (2013) indicate the longevity of the characters (although this fifth *Die Hard* film was judged a disappointment by both critics and fans, in part for its departure from the formula of the earlier films). Both *Rambo: First Blood Part II* and the original *Die Hard* significantly influenced the development of the genre. Both also generated extensive critical commentary. Indeed following the emergence of such 1980s action franchises, scholars began to engage with action cinema in a detailed way that only the Western had received to that date (and then largely without reference to the significance of action).

Rambo: First Blood Part II was a major commercial success, a block-buster of an order that seemed to require comment at a time when budgets for action films were rapidly escalating (Rambo's production budget was approximately $44 million, perhaps double that of *Raiders of the Lost Ark* a few years previously). Itself a sequel – as the title suggests – to 1982's *First Blood*, the film elevated the Vietnam veteran from troubled victim to heroic savior figure for the Reaganite era. The commercial success of *Die Hard* in turn generated a series of imitators and shifted the tone of the action blockbuster towards a breezy ironic mode that framed the violent spectacle on offer in new ways. While Rambo is an embittered, muscular veteran of the Vietnam War, *Die Hard*'s John McClane is a displaced New York City cop, an everyman figure and emblematic regular guy.

However different (and that difference is itself significant, given a tendency to homogenize the genre), in related ways these characters and the film franchises in which they featured were central to developing critical debates around the action cinema. While popular reviews expressed uncertainty as to the trend, fearing (not for the first time) that spectacle had displaced narrative and thematic complexity, scholars employed the films to highlight issues of masculinity and male images as well as the significance of racial hierarchies in popular representation.

Rambo, the Vietnam Veteran and Masculinity in 1980s Action

The character of John Rambo was introduced in a book, *First Blood* written by David Morrell and first published in 1972. Adapted as *First Blood* a decade later, the role provided Stallone's first major success after his breakthrough role as Rocky, an unknown Philadelphian boxer who has a chance to fight the world champion and goes the distance. Stallone's association with the underdog who wins through certainly informs *First Blood* in which Rambo is a persecuted as well as an asocial figure. The film also played off what was a familiar stereotype for movie audiences in the 1970s and 1980s, that of the Vietnam veteran as homeless drifter who is prone to violence and even psychosis (Martin Scorsese's 1973 *Taxi Driver* is surely the best known American film to feature such an unravelling male protagonist). Considering the decade's other high profile action franchises, we might note that policeman hero Martin Riggs, played by Mel Gibson in the *Lethal Weapon* films, is also a Vietnam veteran. Riggs' backstory as a suicidal risk-taker explicitly stems from his acute grief following the death of his wife, but is framed by pervasive cultural associations of unstable veterans.

In *First Blood* John Rambo wanders into the small town of Hope and, because his face doesn't fit, becomes ensnared in an escalating confrontation with local sheriff Teasle (Brian Dennehy). Rambo escapes police custody – in the process revealing his martial skills – taking refuge in the neighboring woods. The latter part of the film is then composed of a fast-paced account of his ability to hunt down the police and soldiers who attempt to pursue him. Rambo is unable to explain himself and has relatively little dialogue in the film, emphasizing his isolation from others. The arrival of Rambo's former commanding officer, Colonel Trautman (Richard Crenna) makes the character's backstory explicit. Trautman effectively explains Rambo to both the cops and the audience in the cinema (already party to flashbacks of torture and trauma during the police station scenes). Trautman announces himself with the line: "God didn't make Rambo, I made him." Whether he is cast as a Frankenstein's monster (made by a military mentor), a "psycho" or a malfunctioning machine ("one of your machines blew a gasket" observes a furious Teasle), these analogies construct Rambo as inhuman in some fundamental way. Indeed Rambo's ability to thrive in the natural habitat more effectively than in the town suggests an animal or primitive character. As Studlar and Desser suggest, iconographic elements such as the bow and arrow associating Rambo with native Americans, while his iconic whiteness (and that of the POWs he rescues) elides the racial hierarchies of the American military during the Vietnam war itself. The appropriation of an imagery of the "noble savage" works, they suggest, to qualify though never completely

PLATE 8.1 The action hero is pictured as both natural predator and manufactured warrior in *Rambo: First Blood Part II* (1985, directed by George P. Cosmatos and produced by Anabasis N.V.)

displace the by then familiar cinematic designation of the veteran as "psychopathic misfit." Rambo's capacity for guerrilla warfare (an important narrative element in all the films to date) aligns him with a defensive rather than aggressive military strategy, yet his "sheer implacability and indestructability" suggest the opposite (1990: 109).

At the conclusion of *First Blood*, having brought destruction to the small American town, Rambo ultimately breaks down in front of Trautman, tearfully speaking of his isolation and the memories that haunt him. If the first film's narrative seemed to unfold around the revelation of the violence, danger and implacable character of the central character, *Rambo: First Blood Part II* exaggerated these characteristics. Rambo's explosive qualities are harnessed for an official mission to seek evidence of prisoners of war. The move suggests that his violence can be used and controlled by the government as well as pointing to what was a touchstone issue of the era (American soldiers, now POWs formed the basis of the *Missing in Action* series starring former karate champion Chuck Norris). *Rambo* was one of a number of films that revisited the Vietnam War, forming part of a new visibility for veterans. Vietnam did not typically appear in Hollywood genre films, although the war's traumatic violence shaped the critically renowned New Hollywood epics *Apocalypse Now!* (1979) and *The Deer Hunter* (1978). While a Vietnam War film such as *Hamburger Hill* (1987) recycled the conventions of the World War II movie (e.g., military pride overcoming ethnic/racial and other differences), it also incorporated a now familiar sense of distance from those in charge, military authorities whose orders result in huge casualties for seemingly little strategic gain.

Rambo became notorious for the line, uttered by Stallone as Trautman gives him the offer of the mission and thus secures his release from hard labor: "Do we get to win this time?" (Trautman's response "This time it's up to you" accords the hero both agency and responsibility. The line lays the blame for American defeat in Vietnam not with the military but squarely with the government. Indeed such a scenario will be re-enacted as Rambo, having found POWs is abandoned by the representatives of the government. Having battled to the top of a hill with a bedraggled POW, Rambo is almost aboard a helicopter when it is ordered to withdraw. The subsequent aerial image of the two men surrounded by advancing Vietnamese troops powerfully visualizes the betrayal while recalling the costly capture of high ground that forms the basis of so many war movies.

For many critics, Rambo's declaration of a desire to win points to the deep conservatism of the 1980s action cinema, replaying a notorious American military defeat as spectacular triumph. The film's alignment of Vietnamese with Soviet forces responds to what were contemporary US concerns (the new Cold War) at the same time as they evoked the conventions of an earlier era. Rambo's extraordinary fighting abilities – his ability to embody war – suggests that in fantastical form America can indeed achieve. Taking and overcoming on his Soviet and Vietnamese captors, Rambo survives brutal torture in order (once again) to violently confront Murdoch, a representative of specifically American/US authority.

Indeed Rambo exemplifies what Susan Jeffords influentially termed the hard-bodied heroes of action cinema. For Jeffords both the "hard-body imaginary" that typified the Reagan presidency and the display of "physical prowess" in the *Rambo* films speak to a rejection of the supposed weakness of the Carter years, expressing nationalist pride through images of renewed masculinity. The officials against which Rambo (fictionally) and Reagan (rhetorically and legislatively) pitted themselves are seen to weaken the nation. The star body of the action hero is crucial to Jeffords argument. She writes: "The true success of *First Blood*, both symbolically and as a marketing tool, is to have created the desire in citizens/audiences to see more bodies like Rambo's, an achievement to which the blockbuster films of the 1980s can attest" (1993: 34). For Jeffords then, the action cinema as it develops through the 1980s and into the 1990s speaks to a desire for images of male strength, images that perform ideological work of recuperation in American cultural life.

This chapter's epigraph, "*Rambo* seems to be on everyone's mind these days," is eminent critic Andrew Sarris's observation on the urgent need to take a view on the film.[1] To some extent the political

---

[1] The renowned auteur critic adds "people don't seem to have to see it to hate it (or what it stands for, whatever that is)." While he is no enthusiast, he aims to put the film in perspective and focuses on what he regards as inappropriate attempts to judge Stallone on the basis of his lack of military service rather than any other criteria. (Sarris, 1985: 53)

controversies surrounding *Rambo* at the time of its release, and the subsequent scholarly readings of the film as symptomatic of an era, tended to obscure the film's significance in genre terms – both its relationship to past forms and its redefinition of those forms via an emphasis on the spectacle of the star body and an intensified violence more often associated with realist war movies to that point. Thomas Doherty aligns *Rambo* with the three Chuck Norris *Missing in Action* movies (1984, 1985, 1988), all of which he deems to be "fanciful action-adventures" that, taken together, serve as evidence that "the rollicking matinee spirit lives" (1999: 286–287). *Time* magazine noticed that alongside the evocation of Vietnam, "Rambo has echoes of half a dozen movie heroes of old, from Tarzan to Shane, and his Vietnamese and Soviet foes are updated versions of the malevolent Japanese and Germans from World War II films" (Zoglin, 1985: 53). While there are certainly commonalities with the adventure films of an earlier era, and indeed those of the same era, *Rambo* stood out for critics and its contemporary audiences as rather different in both kind and degree.

Clearly the film incorporates core adventure cinema elements (heroism, adventure in spectacular landscapes, diverse forms of conflict and peril, extraordinary physical endeavors) but it eschews the lighthearted tone that characterized adventure cinema in favor of the tough approach delivered in gritty urban action films such as *Dirty Harry*. Like *Dirty Harry*, there is a thorough-going skepticism as to the integrity of officials and politicians. In the Eastwood film, San Francisco's mayor is constantly seeking to ameliorate rather than confront the vicious killer Scorpio. In *Rambo* the hero is framed by betrayal. Vietnam is presented as a war lost by politicians rather than servicemen. In that rhetorical play the hero's body and its capacity to absorb punishment and dispense death is crucial.

The display of the male body was central to *Rambo* and to its promotion, Stallone's physique considerably enlarged for the movie in comparison to earlier roles. The association of the half-naked figure of Rambo with both nature and weaponry is captured in the film's posters, the hero brandishing a rocket-launcher against a fiery background. While Jeffords argued that there was a desire for such bodies, representing national strength, many reviewers mocked the spectacle that was deemed overblown and even grotesque. The display of the body suggested to some critics a masculinity that needed to assert itself, disavowing the potential for homoeroticism via excessive violence.

The coupling of the heroic body on display and screen violence is most evident in the matched figures of the tortured/damaged and the avenging hero. Scenes of torture feature prominently not only in *Rambo* (in which torture functions as one part of the film's broader spectacle while developing the narrative), but in other prominent action movies, notably *Lethal Weapon* and *The Long Kiss Goodnight*. In *Die Hard*, the hero's body is the site of violence, a sign of his resilience and the brutality of the enemies he opposes. Doherty concedes that *Rambo* is "deft" in its use of these themes, writing: "For all its violence and butchery, *Rambo* confirmed the vital cultural function of Hollywood genre: to ease division and reconcile conflict through myth" (1999: 292).

My own work has emphasized the connections between a muscular body and class, with muscles signifying physical labor. *Spectacular Bodies* further relates the class discourse of Rambo to the populist, anti-government thrust of the films that position a spectacular everyman betrayed by officialdom: "The action cinema depends on a complex articulation of both belonging and exclusion, an articulation which is bound up in the body of the hero and the masculine identity that it embodies" (Tasker, 1993: 8). Contemporary critics may well have responded with discomfort to the decorative function of the muscular male body in 1980s action movies, a response that shifted as the commodified male image took center stage with the prominence of stars such as Brad Pitt. The repeated reference in contemporary writings to audiences becoming too involved, cheering the action suggests anxiety of a different sort – one which has long accompanied the cinema with its promise of illicit representation. Several scholars, however, position the muscular hero as an ambivalent figure rather than a straightforward endorsement of nationalist or masculinist ideologies; the scenarios in which he features read as playing out themes of power and powerlessness that have undoubted popular appeal. The "physical struggles for self-control and for control over one's body" (Tasker, 1993: 126) that are played out in action movies function at a dramatic and a metaphorical level perpetually pointing to capacity for action/movements and the constraints placed around that capacity.

In line with the overview of action in the opening chapters of this book, I'd like to end this section by foregrounding formal qualities as an aspect of *Rambo*'s success and its influence on the genre. Violence is central to the spectacle in *Rambo*, an element of the visual impact that has come to characterize the action cinema and to escalate the budgets required to deliver such movies on a blockbuster scale. Yet the film's visual style is less often discussed than its ideological emphasis. Writes the *Village Voice*'s J. Hoberman: "*Rambo* begins with an explosion, and that voluptuous, rolling fireball – molten gold, lava orange – is reprised again and again during the fiery climax" (1985: 66). To describe fire as voluptuous conveys something of the sensuous quality that writers would later describe as the core of action spectacle, its visceral character particularly suited to large screens. This spectacle of ever larger weapons, bodies and explosions characterizes the hyperbolic action film that thrived during the 1980s and which has continued to form a component of the contemporary action blockbuster. In the 1980s action becomes prominently established as a genre of excess, its heroes are figures of strength pitted against seemingly overwhelming odds.

Die Hard, the Everyman Hero and Spaces of Action

Die Hard begins with John McClane, a New York police office, arriving in Los Angeles to visit his estranged wife for Christmas. He is chauffeur driven from the airport – the initial contrast between his regular guy character and the luxury of the limousine gradually undercut by McClane's banter with the driver. The car, like the high rise building in which she works, is a sign of wife Holly's success in business – a success that has taken her to LA and, together with McClane's stubbornness about remaining in New York, thus divided the family. Having set the personal scene of a divided couple who clearly still care about each other, *Die Hard* plunges into action – indeed it is through action that these personal concerns will ultimately be resolved.

The action is triggered when Nakatomi Tower is taken over by a gang of ruthless, technologically equipped and brutal pseudo-terrorists. Under their leader Hans Gruber (Alan Rickman) the gang aim to pull off an elaborate heist under the guise of a terrorist cell – raiding

PLATE 8.2 Extraordinary regular guys: Bruce Willis' wisecracking cop hero John McClane in *Die Hard* (1988, directed by John McTiernan and produced by Twentieth Century Fox Film Corporation, Gordon Company and Silver Pictures).

the company vaults while buying time by demanding the release of political prisoners from a number of seemingly random groups. While the Nakatomi staff are held hostage and the security guard killed, McClane eludes capture. Roaming the building – several floors of which remain under construction – McClane causes havoc, uncovering the true goal of Gruber's gang and proceeding to foil them at every turn. Through tactical battles, intimidation, gunfights and one-on-one combat, ultimately McClane defeats the gang, saves Holly and the two are reunited at the film's close. Violence is both punishing and redemptive in this scenario, the hero apologizes for his mistakes and overcomes his enemies.

Die Hard centers on McClane's tough cop, a role that took actor Bruce Willis from being largely a television star (primarily his role as wisecracking private detective in the action comedy *Moonlighting*) to a mainstay of the action movie. Despite the ever more elaborate stunts performed by McClane over the course of the *Die Hard* films, the character remains defined as an everyman figure, a regular guy. In contrast to many other action heroes of 1980s cinema, he has no military background to accord him veteran status, or access to specialist knowledge. Of course like other action heroes from Harry Callaghan to the comic action cops played by Jackie Chan and Chris Tucker in the *Rush Hour* series (1998, 2001, 2007), he has cop knowledge and experience on which to draw. Familiar with violence, able to follow hunches, to seize opportunities and think on his feet, McClane's police hero achieves extraordinary feats by using what comes to hand: parcel tape to strap a handgun to his back, a firehose round his waist to leap from the burning roof, strapping explosives to a computer monitor and dispatching them down an elevator shaft.

McClane characterizes himself as a "fly in the ointment." It is vital to both his characterization and to the plot that McClane is not meant to be in the building when it is attacked. His presence is as an estranged husband, more or less officially erased as Holly Genarro is using her own rather than her married name. Although a police officer he has no authority in LA; his expertise is required and yet repeatedly rejected by the local police chief and the FBI. The action hero who finds himself operating in opposition to authority would be a recurrent feature of the film and of the 1980s action cinema. While the soldier and police heroes of earlier decades may bridle at (and then make the best of) the situations in which they are placed by their superiors, McClane must confront not only the terrorists but also the rigid stupidity of the LAPD and the FBI. Moreover, in contrast to earlier films featuring maverick or rogue heroes, McClane is literally detached from police or military authority. Only Sergeant Al Powell (Reginald Veljohnson) supports him, offering comfort and information over the radio. During a conversation between the two, McClane admits to feeling "unappreciated," his efforts unwelcome to the authorities who, taking everything at face value, are unable to grasp the complexity of the situation with which they are dealing. For the audience, however, aware of the gang's true objective and the necessity of the race against time, McClane is the uncontroversial hero; the authorities a bothersome distraction from action.

McClane is literally and metaphorically besieged: in this he has been read as a sign of blue collar frustration, expressing rage at a corporate culture for which the building stands. The systematic destruction of the building from the elegance of the Christmas party to the chaos of explosive flames and broken glass certainly supports such an argument. McClane's opposition to inept authorities and to slick corporate criminals as well as his more obviously successful professional wife is cited in numerous essays that typically read *Die Hard* as evidence of the cultural conservatisms of 1980s America (the rejection of authority, for example, suggesting a dysfunctional system). Jeffords positions McClane with John Rambo and Martin Riggs of the *Lethal Weapon* films as "the new heroes of the Reagan era" (1993: 63), railing at bureaucracy and the consequences of feminism. Jeffrey A. Brown suggests that *Die Hard* forms part of a distinctive "action-cop genre" one which operates as a "mythic wish-fulfilment of the American dream" (1993: 87). Brown sees the film as part of a group with which it has formal and ideological elements in common. However, the very diversity of action genres, historically and within a particular decade such as the 1980s, means that *Die Hard* can be (legitimately) positioned within more than one trend. It looks back – affectionately – to the Western, evokes the disaster movie and jungle adventure, as well as sharing iconographic elements with warrior action, popularly associated at that time with stars such as van Damme, Schwarzenegger, Seagal and Stallone.

Some critics read *Die Hard* as presenting another indestructible hero: so Martin Flanagan suggests that: "Despite the pretensions of McClane and Traven [Keanu Reeves' character in *Speed*], we are in no doubt as to their heroic credentials as soon as we are introduced to them" (2004: 109). While this is certainly the case, it is worth noting that neither Willis nor Reeves was associated with action roles at the time when *Die Hard* and *Speed* were first released – indeed for contemporary audiences the casting seemed unlikely. Lichtenfeld effectively captures the distinctive quality of McClane's action hero when he writes:

> What makes this war so compelling is that the film's imagery and screenplay and Willis's performance (vulnerable, regretful, wise-cracking from exasperation, not with other action heroes' ironic detachment) make McClane an everyman, of whom producer Lawrence Gordon says, "He seems to be a man that you believe could lose". (2007: 165)

And while it would certainly be possible to argue that McClane/Willis's vulnerability is merely another expression of beleaguered white masculinity, *Die Hard* achieves its effect in large part due to this tension, this possibility that the hero will not succeed even as audiences are aware that he surely will. The work, indeed the sheer effort, involved in getting to the inevitable victory is displayed through McClane's damaged body and his increasingly ragged appearance. Shot at, feet bloodied from walking over broken glass and bruised from a punishing fight with Karl, McClane is an embodiment of violence in all senses.

Lichtenfeld argues that *Die Hard* was not only hugely commercially successful but that it became "a template for the next decade's action films" (2007: 161). That template involved exploiting the possibilities of a confined space of action coupled with the spectacular destruction of that scene of action whether a building, plane, stadium, ship and so on. These confined spaces involve a particular intense delivery of the function Flanagan takes from literary theorist Bakhtin to describe action cinema, "enforced movement through space" (2004: 108). Events happen to the 1980s Hollywood action hero: he (or occasionally she) does not typically seek out action despite being clearly equipped to tackle its challenges.

The hero responds by demonstrating an intuitive understanding of space (and this is as true of the expanded space in which Rambo, discussed previously, operates). As Flanagan observes, "McClane evades capture by achieving an instinctive, intimate understanding of the layout of the building, using its secondary structures (access tunnels, air vents) to move around in" (2004: 114). These are also, of course, precisely the spaces invisible to the elite corporate users of the building, so that McClane's ability to use these areas to his advantage underlines his difference from both "terrorists" and business people. Surviving trial by fire and water – the elegant lobby of the Nakotomi Corporation rendered a hellish war movie location with Willis aping Rambo's adaption to the natural environment as he shelters from the flames in an ornamental fountain: *Die Hard* betrays both the generic roots and future direction of American action cinema.

CHAPTER 9

GLOBAL AND POSTMODERN ACTION: *CROUCHING TIGER, HIDDEN DRAGON* (2000) AND *KILL BILL* (2003)

It is undoubtedly the case that American filmmaking has long been shaped through transnational exchanges, whether of styles, performers or other personnel. Since at least the 1970s, the influence of diverse Asian action traditions has had a considerable impact both on filmmaking and on scholarship. The dependence on international markets to secure profits for Hollywood films in the action adventure mode has also been increasingly apparent. Christina Klein goes so far as to claim that "Hollywood is becoming Asianized in diverse ways, while Asian film industries are in turn becoming Hollywoodized" (2004: 361). Klein's remarks, made in the wake of the success of Ang Lee's *Crouching Tiger, Hidden Dragon*, foreground financial exchanges in the form of co-productions, the movement of personnel and the location of filming in a range of national sites as well as the patterns of exchange and influence between national filmmaking styles.

The Hollywood Action and Adventure Film, First Edition. Yvonne Tasker.
© 2015 John Wiley & Sons, Inc. Published 2015 by John Wiley & Sons, Inc.

Klein's analysis of an Asianized Hollywood emphasizes formal influences exercised by a mobile workforce:

> When the Wachowski brothers hired Hong Kong martial-arts choreographer-extraordinaire Yuen Wo-ping to take charge of the action scenes in *The Matrix*, they radically transformed the visual style of the American action film – and brought it into closer aesthetic affiliation with the contemporary Hong Kong action film. (2004: 368)

The Matrix certainly impressed audiences and influenced filmmakers through its play with speed and its innovative fight choreography. The rapidity with which *The Matrix* was parodied serves as a marker of its cultural resonance. Nonetheless, that pattern of incorporating formal elements and personnel from other national cinemas has been a longstanding feature of Hollywood genre cinema.

Transnational exchanges are by definition multiple. Cinematic exchanges between Europe and the United States, for example, operate on a number of levels, from settings, to personnel and genre. Chapter 4 noted the popularity of Merrie England as a setting for Hollywood films of the 1930s and 1940s. Travelling in the opposite direction, American urban *noir* and gangster films clearly impacted on French New Wave filmmakers as exemplified by Godard's *À bout de souffle* (1961) or Melville's *Le Samouraï* (1967); films that in turn influenced a generation of American filmmakers. European performers from Arnold Schwarzenegger to Jason Statham have taken up action roles in Hollywood films, while European directors such as Ridley Scott have built careers in American action filmmaking.

The Western has proven to be a remarkably mobile genre, generating waves of production in Germany and, most visibly in international markets, Italy. Sergio Leone's films made a star of American actor Clint Eastwood, a figure who has remained very much associated with the American Western. Looking past Leone to the wider industrial context and less well known examples of Italian Westerns, Dimitris Eleftheriotis writes of "an eclectic engagement with the American Western that demonstrates both an awareness of the national specificity of the latter and a desire to overcome and evade national ideologies and histories" (2004: 313). Eleftheriotis cites Bazin's 1950s writings on the Western and his perplexity as to the evident interest of international audiences in a genre so fascinated with specifically American history. Yet for a trope to be meaningful in a different national context than that which generated it – whether it is particular way of shooting a fight scene or the desert landscape – does not depend on cultural understanding. Indeed for some critics Hollywood cinema has borrowed elements from Asian action in a superficial and even stereotypical manner.

This chapter discusses two films – both box office and, to different degrees, critical hits – which have been widely discussed in the context of transnational or global action: *Crouching Tiger, Hidden Dragon* (2000) and *Kill Bill* (2003, 2004). Both are hybrid works, and both have attracted critical interest for their centering of female fighters as well as the questions of transnational film culture that they exemplify. Long a byword for conservative blockbuster filmmaking, the appearance of visually distinctive action films such as *Crouching Tiger, Hidden Dragon* and *Kill Bill* coincided with developing scholarly interest in the aesthetics, and the aesthetic possibilities, of action. In very different ways then, these two titles point to some significant shifts in the cultural and critical status of action genres.

Transnational Action: Crouching Tiger, Hidden Dragon

Directed by Ang Lee, the American-Chinese-Hong Kong and Taiwanese co-production, *Crouching Tiger, Hidden Dragon* not only secured audiences worldwide, but was a dominating presence at that year's awards season. The film played extensively at festivals as well as multiplexes, bringing action to a wider range of western audiences than was typical and attracting popular audiences to a foreign language film, notoriously difficult in the United States. And while action films routinely win awards in categories in those areas – such as sound editing and visual effects – in which the genre has long been at the forefront of innovation, Lee's film was regarded as aesthetically innovative, securing numerous awards in high prestige categories such as direction, cinematography and screenplay. This is not to say that the film was critically uncontested, with some writers suggesting it was inauthentic in its presentation of Asian action for western audiences.

Producer James Schmaus characterized *Crouching Tiger* as a "pan-Chinese" production due to the range of national contexts from which it drew finance and personnel (Kemp, 2000: n.p.). As an action film the pace of *Crouching Tiger, Hidden Dragon* is slow. Although it is punctuated by a significant number of complex fight and spectacle sequences, each carefully timed to punctuate and illuminate narrative development, *Crouching Tiger* opts for an, at times, wistful tone. Without the explosions and aggressive sound editing that had come to be associated with the action genre, *Crouching Tiger, Hidden Dragon* is formally distinct from both the Chinese swordplay traditions that it reworks and the American action cinema against which it was juxtaposed in western cinemas. At a thematic level, the film's foregrounding of the emotional life of the central characters, shaped by themes of duty and honor, represented a distinctive melancholy tone. Visually, the emphasis on landscape, period detail and on visual composition aligned *Crouching Tiger* with art cinema conventions more than those of action cinema.

PLATE 9.1 The striking visual compositions in *Crouching Tiger, Hidden Dragon* draw on numerous sources including the action cinema's dynamic framing of combat and an evocation of the natural world more often associated with art cinema: Li Mu Bai (Chow Yun Fat) (*Wo Hu Cang Long*, 2000, directed by Ang Lee and produced by Asia Union Film & Entertainment Ltd., China Film Co-Production Corporation, Columbia Pictures Film Production Asia, EDKO Film, Good Machine, Sony Pictures Classics, United China Vision and Zoom Hunt International Productions Company Ltd).

Crouching Tiger, Hidden Dragon centers on the conflicts and connections between its principle characters. Chow Yun-Fat and Michelle Yeoh play fighters, Li Mu Bai and Shu Lien, whose intense love for each other is both repressed and yet visible to all. Their manner is stiff and formal; fluidity of movement is evident only when they are training or fighting, images that contradict an otherwise restrained or even repressed self-presentation. Such characters are in some respects archetypal; the figure of the fighter who represses emotions in pursuit of duty is a familiar one across genres, periods and national cinemas. The events of the narrative are initiated by Li Mu Bai's decision to give up his sword, the Green Destiny, and implicitly the life of repression with which it is associated. This ancient and powerful weapon serves as an over-determined symbol of authority; through the course of the film it is variously given, stolen (more than once), returned and cast aside.

If Li Mu Bai initiates the events by giving up the sword, in the process exploring the possibility of a different life, Jen Yu/Yu Jiaolong (Zhang Ziyi)'s theft of the sword signals her desire for an alternative mode of existence.[1] The daughter of an aristocratic family, Jen Yu is extraordinarily accomplished and ill disciplined, restless and restrained. She is also about to be married, a prospect for which she has little enthusiasm; instead she expresses admiration for Shu Lien and the freedom of a fighter's life. The extent to which the sword is fetishized underlines the rebelliousness of stealing it; Jen Yu appropriates power and status. That process is clearly laid out in the teahouse fight sequence, in the prelude to which the newly minted fighter stakes a claim to public recognition, asserting that she has defeated Li Mu Bai. This rebellion echoes that of Jen Yu's mentor, Jade Fox (Cheng Pei Pei) whose bitterness at her exclusion leads to violence and to her

---

[1] Stephen Teo notes that the English subtitles change the name of Zhang Ziyi's character for reasons of accessibility. Moreover, he notes that "Her Chinese name resonates with two important motifs of the story: her family name, Yu, meaning Jade, associates her with the Green Destiny sword, while her given name, Jiaolong, meaning 'tender dragon,' identifies her as the 'Hidden Dragon' of the title" (2005: 202–203).

attempts to usurp authority. Jade Fox is a figure of abjection, fuelled by rage and disempowered by her inability to read the secret book she has stolen; an outlaw figure who must hide herself, she is clearly opposed to the restraint that defines Shu Lien and Li Mu Bai. She is responsible for the poisoning of the latter's master, triggering a quest for revenge. Having subverted Jade Fox's training (which she long ago surpassed), Jen Yu/Yu Jiaolong will reject Li Mu Bai's offer that she become his apprentice, thereby rejecting the constraints of the fighter. The film's themes of, in Ang Lee's words, "social obligation versus personal freedom" suffuse these stories with a particularly gendered inflection of the meaning of restraint and the freedom to move or act in the world (Kemp, 2000: n.p.). Within this frame violence and action can function as a mark of rebellion (Jen Yu's illicit skills and her illicit affair with bandit Dark Cloud Lo [Chen Chang]) and as evidence of obedience or discipline. The film's action aesthetic is centered on character movement, employing wire work for aerial combat (with the final confrontation taking place, by contrast, below ground) and shots of the action from above and below. The visual freedom of movement suggests the broader themes with which the film is concerned.

Before *Crouching Tiger*, director Ang Lee was best known to western audiences for his elegant family pieces *Eat Drink Man Woman* and, more widely, for *Sense and Sensibility* (1995), his first American film. Subsequently he would describe *Crouching Tiger* as "Sense and Sensibility with martial arts" – what seemed a joking reference to the middle-brow Austen adaptation captured the mix of female-centered period drama that the film offers. While it is certainly an action film, Lee's "high aesthetic sensibility" (in film critic Philip Kemp's words) takes *Crouching Tiger* in other directions. It seems clear that the film frustrated Chinese audiences, although its success in western and Asian markets demonstrated the possibilities and, significantly, the potential aesthetic and commercial benefits of co-production. A transnational film that used but also reframed familiar generic elements, *Crouching Tiger*'s success, writes Kenneth Chan, "evoked suspicions of stereotyping, exoticism, traditionalism, and pandering to a Western gaze" (2004: 4). Chan cites Lee's own description of *Crouching Tiger* as "a kind of dream of China, a China that probably never existed," arguing that the film "uses traditional myths and cinematic conventions to create a fantasy space" (2004: 7) in which those same myths are called into question.

In both packaging Chinese culture for western audiences and simultaneously seeking to complexly subvert (rather than reproduce) martial arts conventions, *Crouching Tiger* demonstrated the rich possibilities of transnational action.

Postmodern Action: Kill Bill

Released in two parts in 2003 and 2004, Quentin Tarantino's *Kill Bill* exemplifies a postmodern cinema of pastiche, incorporating numerous references to and borrowings from an eclectic range of filmmaking periods, styles and stars. These references are both superficial and meaningful. Thus, for example, the visual allusion to Bruce Lee's final unfinished film pointedly expressed through the Bride's (Uma Thurman) yellow costume – an image widely used in promoting *Kill Bill* – signifies the character's status as a skilled fighter and the ability to take on larger or seemingly more skilled opponents. The complex issues of power and status raised by the association of Lee as a Hong Kong/Hollywood martial arts star and Uma Thurman as a white western actor associated with unconventional female roles, in part due to her stature, are not central to *Kill Bill* in the way that the image might suggest. Nonetheless, the prominence of the association is provocative, insisting on a relationship between the American protagonist and an icon of Asian action, just as the casting of David Carradine as Bill refers to an earlier decade's appropriation of martial arts genres via his most famous role as Kwai Chang Caine in the television series *Kung Fu* (ABC, 1972–1975).

The global character of action cinema became increasingly apparent in the twenty-first century. Indeed the postmodern tone of *Kill Bill* stems in large part from Tarantino's hybrid style, a self-conscious incorporation of references to and elements from a range of national action cinemas – including those of Hong Kong, Japan and Hollywood. The referential texture of *Kill Bill* is meaningful above all in calling attention to the film's status as a hybrid action movie, its heightened invitation to view the events onscreen as not only spectacular but as spectacularly self-aware. While Schmaus, as we have seen, described *Crouching Tiger* as pan-Chinese, *Kill Bill* aspires to enact a form of pan-action. In its form and in its production, it exemplifies both transnational and postmodern action. The film was shot in part in China, a move that Klein reads as both positive and negative, "taking advantage of China's inexpensive yet skilled film workers" (2004: 368). It draws together fighting, film styles and locations from America, Hong Kong and Japan. The hybrid style – featuring abrupt shifts in tone and setting – as well as the episodic, fractured narrative is particularly associated with Tarantino and to this extent was already familiar territory for audiences following major commercial successes such as *Pulp Fiction* (1994). Yet the success of the film speaks to the early twenty-first century currency of those diverse action tropes and genres (some modern, some not) exploited in *Kill Bill*.

Kill Bill is one of a number of high profile American films and television series in the 2000s to foreground violent female protagonists often according them aptitude in martial arts. O'Day's (2004) designation of this trend as "action babe cinema" refers to the presentation of the female form as one part of the larger action spectacle, coupling a semi-pornographic interest in women's bodies with an aesthetic emphasis on the body in motion that characterizes action. *Kill Bill* has been extensively discussed in action scholarship and is frequently cited as an example of postmodern cinema. Lisa Coulthard also analyzes *Kill Bill* as an example of postfeminist film culture, a contention she grounds in the film's particular presentation of female violence and violence against women.

Kill Bill opens with a shocking image of such violence; from a black screen over which we hear strained breathing to a close up of The Bride/Beatrice Kiddo, her face battered and bloody. The Bride's fear and pain is filmed in black and white. Former mentor Bill's words are heard as he tenderly wipes her face before shooting her in the head, cutting off her revelation that she is carrying his baby with the shot taking us abruptly to the film's title card. The events leading up to that shocking moment of violence and the consequences that unfold following it are revealed during the course of the two films. In the process the culturally burdened images of the pregnant bride, the eroticized assassin and the female victim of sexual violence are played out around Thurman's character. Kiddo's quest for vengeance – both for the loss of her child (that she believes dead but with whom she is later reunited) and the sexual/physical violence done to her body – organizes the film. At times it is furious, at other times cold, yet Kiddo is absolutely implacable. Although *Kill Bill* achieves a certain dark humor through its references and through the excess of its images of violence, Kiddo's action and her violence is not in itself either comical or sexualized as is so often the case in films of the period. Rather, her determination and her martial skills are consistently foregrounded.

Violence is fundamental to the impact of *Kill Bill* as an action film, suffusing the narrative and taking many forms; it is intimate and spectacular, both humorously gory and a source of aesthetic pleasure. Bodies are variously shot, slashed, pierced, smashed and mangled. Questions of violence and representation would be brought to the fore for discussions of *Kill Bill*, as they had been for earlier Tarantino films, notably his debut as director, *Reservoir Dogs* (1992). Just as *Crouching Tiger* is an action film that uses the pace more often associated with art cinema, *Kill Bill* couples the conventions of action with the unexpected juxtapositions of independent cinema. Geoff King characterizes the film as exemplifying the aesthetic and commercial strategies of "indiewood," appealing to a range of viewers through references to an array of popular cultural sources. Analyzing the fight with Vernita Green (Vivica Fox), King describes *Kill Bill*'s style as coupling "overtly stylized effects" with "an aesthetic designed to create an impression of painful impact and immediacy" (2009: 116–117). The film's immediacy is connected intimately to its violence. While the fight scenes themselves are clearly stylized, an insistence on the visceral

PLATE 9.2 Postmodern action: the Bride (Uma Thurman) confronts multiple antagonists and fighting styles in the richly allusive *Kill Bill* (2003, directed by Quentin Tarantino and produced by Miramax Films, A Band Apart and Super Cool ManChu).

nature of violence – the gushing blood and exaggerated sounds of weapons – is fundamental to *Kill Bill*'s success as an action film.

Aesthetic innovations around the representation of violence have been important to the action cinema for decades. A much cited example in this regard is *Bonnie and Clyde*, with its visceral climax in which the Barrow gang is mown down by machine guns, the violence on the body rendered graphically by several cameras. As with Peckinpah's *The Wild Bunch* two years later, the film's defenders pointed to a sophisticated use of violent imagery, rejecting criticisms of gratuitous spectacle. The question of whether or not violence is meaningful within the context of a given film or genre is related to – indeed in some senses an extension of – similar questions posed around spectacle. What, critics ask, is the relationship of violence (or spectacle more broadly) to a film's narrative or to the development of core themes? Since action is driven by spectacle, by the pleasures of the visual, it is perhaps unsurprising that such debates are commonplace in relation to action films: is the violence gratuitous? Or is it "something more"? Is the film simply a spectacular ride with minimal complexity or content?

Arguably the dimension of *Kill Bill*'s violence that renders it particularly intriguing is its particular rendition of the female warrior type, both in the intersection and exchange (although clearly hierarchical relationship) between Asian and Hollywood action, and in contrast to the conventions of the period. That *Kill Bill*'s scenes of violence most often turn on the avenging Bride opposed in brutal and yet stylized conflict with another violent woman produces a quite particular effect. The film exploits two of the most common narrative explanations or contexts for female violence: the rape-revenge theme and violent mother. The theme of maternal violence – whether implied or explicit –– has long used to somehow explain female agency, while the rape-revenge sub-genre provided a feminist inflection to issues of women's violence and violence against women. *Kill Bill*, Purse and Coulthard suggest, offers a representation of female violence that serves to question or challenge the eroticized images of action women that had come to the fore in films of the early twenty-first century, the imagery of "action babes." While, Purse notes, *Kill Bill*'s poster evokes the eroticized image of mastery audiences have come to associate with Hollywood action, the opening sequence in which the Bride is battered and symbolically killed offers a challenge, "represent[ing] not only an emphatic contradiction of our 'action babe' expectations, but also a reversal of the conventional first appearance of the action hero as an intact, assured and attractive figure" (2011: 86–87). The violent confrontation between the Bride and Vernita Green and the simultaneously gleeful and intensely visceral destruction of the domestic scene involves a tearing apart of conventional feminine appearances.

Kill Bill's location in relation to Asian cinema is clear enough in its use of martial arts as a framework as well as its multiple borrowing from Japanese, Hong Kong and other national/popular film traditions (including the American sub-genre of rape-revenge). In geographical terms the film follows Kiddo from the American suburbs in which she fights Vernita Green to Japan where, clad in the yellow leathers that provided one of the film's iconic images – she fights O-Ren Ishii (Lucy Lui) in a tranquil snow garden. In *Kill Bill Volume 2*, the Bride's apprenticeship to Pai Mei (Gordon Liu) recalls the themes of tuition and mentoring familiar to action audiences of Asian action. Hollywood films have long too adopted that convention whether explicitly in martial arts narratives such as *The Karate Kid* (1984) or in the training camp scenarios of war movies. These themes of training and mentorship are pre-figured in the first film in which Kiddo's revenge is facilitated by seeking out expertise, that of Hattori Hanzo, who crafts an extraordinary sword. For Saša Vojković, "What makes the revenge possible, gives Beatrice Kiddo super-human strength, and conditions the successful achievement of a practically irrational goal, are fighting techniques and strategies that originated in the Far East" (2009: 184).

For Vojković this transnational articulation of the female warrior is a largely positive phenomenon, one in which the "recourse to the space of exile" enables a challenge to the "paternal signifier." Through her psychoanalytic perspective, Vojković argues persuasively that "Tarantino's Beatrice Kiddo engages our capacity to envision a different kind of (especially) female existence, and it is an occasion for alternative subjectivities to come into being" (2009: 188). From a rather different critical perspective, *Kill Bill* has been criticized for an appropriative relationship to Asian cinemas, the re-working of disparate elements read as an inappropriate imposition of a Hollywood perspective. Indeed the dynamic evoked by Vojković of a white western woman's subjectivity achieved through Asian tuition recalls the hierarchies of bi-racial partnerships so common within American action scenarios. Kiddo's mastery of her Asian antagonist, O-Ren Ishii, former member of the Deadly Viper Squad and now a feared mob boss is surely significant in this context. O-Ren's backstory is also that of revenge for violence, the brutal murder of her family; a scenario enacted via anime. Kiddo's confrontation with O-Ren – two powerful warrior women –– is framed in the context of a superior weapon rather than superior swords(wo)manship. Grotesquely and yet cleanly scalped at the culmination of the House of Blue Leaves sequence, O-Ren admires the quality of the sword before collapsing. Having at first disparaged Kiddo's cultural appropriation, O-Ren Ishii retracts that insult prior to her defeat and death. That is, the racial hierarchies that are apparent in this scene – evident also in star Lucy Lui's Chinese-American heritage as well as her association with "action babe" films – are effectively (albeit ironically) confirmed.

Kill Bill has an episodic narrative structure. Through the course of the narrative we learn of the Bride's life as an assassin, a member of the all-female Deadly Viper Assassination Squad. Kiddo's different personas are inscribed with different names and yet the achronological structure ensures that we do not follow a developmental progress; rather the viewer discerns the central character shift and transform from one to another. The film's reference to and recycling of disparate genre sources produces a self-consciously discordant effect, one heightened by an, at times, esoteric use of both music and sound.

Both Purse and Coulthard draw attention to the double register of *Kill Bill*'s interest in female violence. The films are, in Purse's words, "fascinated by the possibilities and problems of displaying female physical violence onscreen" (2011: 90). In juxtaposing scenes of credible, consequential violence with the fantastical and improbable (as in the Bride's slaughter of the Crazy 88s), *Kill Bill* disorients. The contrast between one on one fights and those against multiple antagonists are generically familiar of course. The former are more challenging and intensely motivated, linked in *Kill Bill* to the thread of revenge that runs through and structures the film. How are viewers intended to understand the Bride's violence? Albeit in a very different manner, *Kill Bill* echoes *Crouching Tiger/Hidden Dragon*'s interest in aestheticizing rather than contextualizing violent women. Both are examples of postfeminist action cinema, their relationship to the past – and their strategy of cultural juxtaposition – offering a space in which to imagine their violent female protagonists. As Coulthard observes, *Kill Bill*'s "depiction of female violence is entwined with discourses of idealized feminine whiteness, heterosexuality, victimhood, sacrificial purity, maternal devotion, and eroticized, exhibitionistic, sexual availability" (2007: 158).

It is worth returning to the various promotional images of Thurman as Kiddo, dressed in the yellow outfit that she wears in her spectacular showdown with the Crazy 88's, Gogo and O-Ren Ishii. She holds the sword with which she will wreak revenge. This image evokes not only Lee and Hong Kong cinema but the samurai/swordplay traditions of Chinese and Japanese martial arts. In short the iconic image summons up a generalized depiction of Asian martial arts, embodied in the figure of a thin blonde white woman. *Kill Bill*'s use of tropes including rape/revenge and the maternal avenger rework familiar feminist and postfeminist discourses of female agency. And yet the staging of violence between (as well as against) women, and the formulaic inscription of racial hierarchies, reminds us that postfeminist culture typically works by the deployment of an apolitical evocation of female strength.

CHAPTER 10

ESPIONAGE ACTION: *THE BOURNE IDENTITY* (2002) AND *SALT* (2010)

If action constitutes a genre, it is of a quite diffuse kind. Like the musical and comedy, action acquires its generic character to a great extent by the way in which the story is told, through the foregrounding of visual spectacle, narratives of conflict and themes of heroism, as much as, say, fixed settings or character types. Espionage action – which sits within the broad terrain of the spy thriller – exemplifies this lack of fixity. This chapter explores action movies involving espionage and the government agent as hero, taking as its primary examples *The Bourne Identity* and *Salt*. Both feature extensive action sequences, extrapolating the narrative logic of the chase into scenarios of duplicity, paranoia and conspiracy.

Spy movies do not depend on the sort of intense pace we have come to associate with the action movie. Indeed many films featuring espionage themes are characterized by a relatively slow form of plot development, by sustained suspense and the centralizing of questions

The Hollywood Action and Adventure Film, First Edition. Yvonne Tasker.
© 2015 John Wiley & Sons, Inc. Published 2015 by John Wiley & Sons, Inc.

of identity and trustworthiness: how should actions and events be interpreted? Who can the hero rely on? Can the hero him/herself be trusted? Are those in positions of authority acting with integrity or to serve their own ends? *The Good Shepherd* (2006), which shifts between the protagonist's present and his memories serves as an example. Visually fairly static, the film is centered on unpacking a mystery and tracing a history of sorts; elaborating on the development of the CIA, it typically avoids scenes of action.

Espionage fictions and spy thrillers in the action mode have been a prominent feature of the Hollywood cinema for decades however. The *Mission: Impossible* (1996, 2000, 2006, 2011) and Bourne films (2002, 2004, 2007) are among the most prominent Hollywood franchises. The reinvigoration of the Bond franchise with a tough action emphasis in *Casino Royale* (2006), *Quantum of Solace* (2008) and *Skyfall* (2012) has reinforced the associations of espionage with big-budget film production. Indeed as far back as the 1980s, Bond films had demonstrated the influence of grittier action modes, aware of the need to compete for audiences. Combat scenes in action films revel in making use of the environment, turning unexpected objects into weapons; in the espionage film that inventive violence is an extension of the gadgetry associated particularly with Bond. The elaborate staging of action across different national locations demonstrates the spy hero's mastery of space in exaggerated form.

The proximity of the spy action–adventure movie to comedy or parody has equally been apparent for some years, not least in the 1960s series of Matt Helm movies starring Dean Martin or, arguably, the 1970s James Bond films. The ill-defined private agencies that employ the lead characters as assassins in *Mr & Mrs Smith* (2005) are in this lineage. The film couples action with romantic comedy: in the course of the movie, the bored couple (played by Angelina Jolie and Brad Pitt) will discover each other's secret identities, attempt to kill each other and ultimately form an alliance to defeat a mutual enemy. In the process, their immaculate suburban home is spectacularly destroyed, the final confrontation taking place in a mall. The trope of a secret identity resulting in comic scenarios is deployed routinely in espionage narratives, from *True Lies* (1994) and *The Long Kiss Goodnight* (in which Geena Davis' character is temporarily bewildered by her own abilities) to *Spy Kids* (2001). Thus like the action cinema more broadly, espionage action spans a continuum from light-hearted to intense violence.

Mission: Impossible elaborates a complex, at times incoherent, narrative involving double-crosses and deceit within a community of American spies. While the original series featured a team operating together to pull elaborate cons via illusion and disguise, the films are anchored by Tom Cruise as Ethan Hunt with a decisive shift towards action. Indeed the *Mission: Impossible* films seem designed after the Bond model, situating a definitively American hero in an international action scenario. The relative isolation of Hunt as action hero is underlined in the rapid dispatch of his team in the first film, leaving him "disavowed" by the CIA, a suspect who must work alone to clear his name and uncover the true mole. Hunt is immersed in risky missions that involve danger, spectacular chases and scenes of destruction as well as intrigue. Cruise's role demands a physical performance, recalling the athleticism and physical peril of earlier adventure traditions. Yet while the plot is fairly labyrinthine, in common with the majority of action-oriented spy movies, there is relatively little actual intelligence work in *Mission: Impossible*.

In espionage films such as *Mission: Impossible*, *The Bourne Identity* and *Salt*, the hero is cut off from (and indeed often directly opposed to) official forms of authority. The heroes of all three films/series forge unofficial alliances to assist them in their righteous endeavors. The lone hero is a familiar figure in the action cinema, appearing in several of the films discussed in this book: the populist heroes of *Dirty Harry*, *Rambo* and *Die Hard* are hindered by official forces and those who seek to work too rigidly "by the book," failing to understand the urgency of the threat or unable to read the signs in the way that the hero, armed with experience and extraordinary skills, is able to do. This loner status is also apparent in those variants of the espionage film in which the hero is isolated from, rejected by and under illegitimate surveillance by the forces of the State. In such films the hero may not be an agent at all as, for example, in *Enemy of the State*. A fascination with the surveillance of ordinary citizens/public life is apparent in twenty-first century crime and espionage narratives, with the two often overlapping in the post 9/11 period. A film such as *The Dark Knight* (2008) exploits these concerns, in the process underlining the ambiguity of the Batman character. Espionage scenarios picture the hero as both subject to surveillance and able to use the tools of surveillance technology.

Action Hero as No-Man: The Bourne Identity

In 2002, Universal released *The Bourne Identity*, an adaptation of a Robert Ludlum novel published over 20 years earlier. Directed by Doug Liman, *Bourne* employed a different style to many contemporary action scenarios, notably the superhero and fantasy action films that scored the biggest box office successes that year.[1] Two sequels followed: *The Bourne Supremacy* (2004) and *The Bourne Ultimatum* (2007). These two movies, directed by Paul Greengrass, built on the first film's location work, developing a distinctive quasi-documentary style even as the action intensified in scale. Exploiting a number of European locations along with studio work, *The Bourne Identity* evokes something of the transnational feel of the Bond movies including a set-piece car chase through the streets of Paris. The casting of Matt Damon, who would emerge as an unexpected action star, was certainly a factor in the different feel of the Bourne films. The range of the performances in *The Bourne Identity*, from both leading and supporting actors, and its focus on the drama of a man without an identity quite as much as the action this generates, makes effective use of the narrative and thematic complexity so characteristic of espionage stories.

The Bourne Identity begins with fishermen recovering Bourne's seemingly dead body from stormy seas; the darkness of night and the movement of the small vessel produce a disorienting, claustrophobic feel. Bourne is laid out on the table as if it were a mortuary; only after the vessel's Italian Captain has extracted bullets and an implanted device that reveals the code to a Swiss bank account does the hero revive, instinctively responding to his situation with violence. Asked who he is and why the device was in his hip, Bourne is bewildered,

---

[1] The top four films in the US that year were: *Spider-Man*, *The Lord of the Rings: The Two Towers*, *Star Wars: Episode II – Attack of the Clones* and *Harry Potter and the Chamber of Secrets*. *The Bourne Identity* came in at number 21 for domestic box office.

stumbling around the confined space before collapsing. Though returned from the dead, Bourne does not know who he is. A brief scene takes us to CIA headquarters where a report is given that a mission has failed. The audience is left to infer a connection – the failed mission has something to do with Bourne, but more than that we do not know. In subsequent scenes Bourne's status as part of a secret program is revealed along with the CIA's desire to keep their activities in Africa secret. The contrast between the men (and a few women) in suits and Bourne himself is both marked and generically familiar. Two men, Conklin (Chris Cooper) and Abbott (Brian Cox) confer in secret, their priority following Bourne's failure in his mission is to cover their tracks ensuring their operation is not brought to light. Both at the very top (the Director of the CIA) and at the level of the individual operative (Bourne) there is confusion.

On the fishing vessel that has discovered Bourne, his memory and identity lost, the mystery deepens: Bourne is seen working with the fishermen, exercising, demonstrating his returning fitness and his familiarity with a number of European languages. Palpably distressed at his amnesia, Bourne is put ashore and makes his way to Zurich in order to pursue the only clue he possesses. Here, roused by police as he sleeps on a park bench in the snow, Bourne's aptitude for violence returns to him: he swiftly disarms the two policemen, his face

PLATE 10.1 Jason Bourne's action/espionage identity is a mystery to himself, gradually revealed through an instinctive capacity for violence in *The Bourne Identity* (2002, directed by Doug Liman and produced by Universal Pictures, The Kennedy/Marshall Company, Hypnotic, Kalima Productions GmbH & Co. KG and Stillking Films).

registering uncertainty and surprise but also a sense of recognition as to this new and yet familiar skill. Over the course of the film Bourne will reveal (to us and himself) a detailed knowledge of weaponry and tactics, as well as the ability to navigate urban space undetected. Not until over an hour into the film does the bitter realization that he is an assassin begin to resolve the question of identity for Bourne.

This juxtaposition of a physically powerful man rendered vulnerable by his lack of memory is at the core of *The Bourne Identity*, a particular take on the familiar action trope that casts the outsider hero as an unknown quantity. Unknown to himself, Bourne requires the assistance of an ordinary civilian, Marie (Franka Potente), in order to elude and then confront the forces of the CIA. We've seen already that themes of vulnerability and power are central to the action movie. Bourne's espionage narrative develops these themes in particular ways centering in the first film on Bourne's discovery of his capacity for violence and his assertion of independence. Writing of the action body, Purse emphasizes that the genre perpetually rehearses not only fantasies of empowerment, but of transformation: "fantasies of becoming-powerful, that transitional state where the possibilities of the body are both in the process of being revealed and still full of potential" (2011: 48).

In *The Bourne Identity* this transformation is represented through the hero's increasing ability to master the spaces (and the forces) that seek to contain him. The first of these is the Zurich bank that is depicted as both intimidating and cold. The contrast between the vast empty space of the reception area and the enclosed lift creates a sense of anticipation and tension. The bank sequences use an imagery of bars and steel as well as silent observers suggesting threat and containment for the hero. Bourne's hand is required for identification, building suspense – when no alarm is triggered he moves further into knowledge and danger. The box that is brought to him contains an identity – Jason Bourne, an American who lives in Paris. Hidden beneath are several other passports and identities, contact lens cases, currency and weapons – all the accoutrements of crime or espionage. Taking all but the weapon Bourne refuses the logic of his discovery and action seems to be effectively deferred. While the bank scene conveys clearly that Bourne is being watched and that he is vulnerable, this develops into open conflict only in the American embassy sequence that follows. That is, the space in which Bourne should be safe (as an American) is where violence erupts.

Significantly, although Europe is the scene of violence in *The Bourne Identity*, that disruption originates in the United States. Bourne's helpers are the Italian fisherman and a young German woman who he overhears in the Embassy battling with the bureaucracy to be overcome in securing a visa. Bourne's American passport admits him readily into the Embassy, bypassing the queues that lead outside the building and the Swiss police who are following him. Yet once inside he is newly vulnerable since Americans are his enemies. An increasing mastery of space, an ability to tackle physical and mental challenges underpin the action in the Embassy sequence. Overpowering the military guards, Bourne takes a map of the building from a wall, secures a radio and manages a daring exit scaling the Embassy walls. He once more leaves a gun behind, depositing the gun he has taken in the trash. Here is action as movement made meaningful – Bourne's decisive navigation of space, ability to think creatively and avoid the obvious all speak to the sense of his awakening. The exhilarating speed of the sequence underlines Bourne's capacity for violence as well as his ability to restrain that capacity. The action culminates in Bourne's stealthy and deft descent of the building. He makes his getaway via a human connection however, offering money to Marie (who he knows is in need) in exchange for a lift to Paris.

As Bourne makes his escape, the CIA unit, alerted to his location, springs into action. Here, it is the movement of information that generates speed, accompanied by rapid camera movement and agents talking over each other. Conklin orders a full scale mobilization, ending with the assertion/command/wish: "I want Bourne in a body bag by sundown!" Agents are activated across Europe, seen in their normal lives, professional and seemingly innocuous yet primed for violence. Now the terms of the film are firmly fixed: a manhunt for Bourne, Bourne's quest to uncover his identity, and the need for the operation to remain secret. As the manhunt intensifies, the unit's sinister ability to track the hero becomes apparent. Their investigation, conducted via monitoring communications, security, police and other sources of information, whether public or private, suggests a relentless pursuit. Against this machinery of surveillance, the hero has his knowledge and intuition. His developing relationship with Marie further allows Bourne to articulate his emotions contrasting genuine intimacy to the understanding of identity via spying and theft. During the drive to Paris he has space and time to talk, sleep and think. The pace of the manhunt – the urgent and overlapping dialogue of the CIA unit, the chase elements of the action sequences – contrasts sharply with these more leisurely scenes. This contrast foregrounds the development of a significant relationship between Bourne and Marie – very different to the superficial connections portrayed in numerous Bond films – who will be reunited as a couple at the film's ending.

Marie too becomes subject to CIA surveillance, her likeness reproduced and circulated alongside that of Bourne. Her restless, mobile backstory makes her virtually impossible to pin down: a bill paid here, a phone there but no fixed point of reference. Yet it is through Marie that they are ultimately able to track down Bourne after the couple take shelter in a farmhouse owned by an old boyfriend. Human intimacy thus both imperils and assists the hero of the action film, never more so than in espionage narratives in which deception and the inability to trust are common themes. Bourne's desire to leave violence behind – ultimately he will tell Conklin "I don't want to do this anymore" – is bound up in his human/romantic relationship to Marie. Liman's film reputedly sought to capture the distinctive style of *Run, Lola Run*, a film to which it alluded not least in the casting of Potente as Marie. Both films share a premise of drama organized around action, the urgency requiring an accelerated pace even as the action facilitates more complex personal development.

Marie is sketched as a damaged young woman, her cynical perspective revealed when she tells Bourne: "Nobody does the right thing." Her role develops from spectator to romantic interest and assistant; during the brutal fight between Bourne and a Parisian Treadstone operative sent to kill him, Marie is a horrified spectator. Numb with shock afterwards she must be escorted out of the building. There is a moment of decision immediately before the elaborate car chase sequence that follows in which Bourne, driving Marie's beat up Mini, eludes the Paris police. "Last chance Marie" says Bourne: her decision to stay with him is expressed in an evocative gesture in the context of the genre – buckling up her seatbelt. The movie as ride commences: rock music builds on the soundtrack, along with sirens, screams and screeching tires. Marie's role is once again part spectator – her audible gasp precedes and counterpoints the car crashing into glass.

As an assistant Marie is both capable and creative. Bourne plans an elaborate scheme by which Marie can secure documents from a hotel – as she enters the lobby, his voiceover talks through a complex series of instructions, demonstrating his conviction that the mastery of space will achieve their goal. The camera shows Marie paused, a small figure amidst the opulence of the lobby. Far from being intimidated however, Marie subverts the process (and foregoes the necessity for an action sequence), surprising Bourne by reappearing on the street having simply asked for the records. As she explains, her cover was to say she was the dead man's personal assistant – in effect she profits from the invisibility of woman's supportive role.

Jason Bourne is an assassin created by the CIA. His function is to kill not to gather intelligence, although the latter is what he does through the course of *The Bourne Identity*, gradually coming to understand his own identity in the process. The revelation of Bourne's past repels Marie although their danger binds them together. It means that they must run: "If we stay here, we die." Both are now fugitives, bringing danger and destruction to those they care about. At the farmhouse in which they take shelter Bourne expresses a desire to hide, not to remember the past. Yet the past is in pursuit in the form of an assassin, The Professor (Clive Owen); once Bourne has shot him, the dying man speaks mournfully of their shared experience as part of Treadstone ("We always work alone"). His dying words "look at what they make you give" underline the suppression of emotion and life that violence involves.

As danger intensifies Marie leaves: she will not be a spectator as the film reaches its climax. Bourne appropriates the technology of surveillance to locate the Paris headquarters where he will tackle Conklin. Confronting his CIA past directly, Bourne's memory finally returns – his inability to assassinate a target, deposed African leader Wombosi, who is surrounded by his young children triggered his amnesia. Described by Conklin variously as "a malfunctioning thirty million dollar weapon" and as an example of "behavioral software" gone wrong, Bourne embodies a tension between individual agent and the brutal system that he enables. Indeed, breaking out of the Paris headquarters, Bourne's violence is fully unleashed: having set aside weapons for a good part of the film, now he has a gun in each hand. His escape takes the form of an extraordinary move whereby he uses a corpse to break his fall down the stairwell, expertly shooting an assailant who is advancing up the stairs as he descends.

Conklin tells Bourne that the decision to give up violence is not his to make, implying that both that violence is in his nature and that the investment he represents cannot be simply set aside. While the film's coda in which Bourne and Marie are reunited suggests that he can, the subsequent films involve the past and its violence returning once more. At the beginning of *The Bourne Supremacy*, the pair will be tracked down in India with Marie killed following a pursuit sequence. The film and its sequel follows Bourne waging war on the organization that created him, modifying the original scenario via the figure of CIA Agent Pamela Landy (Joan Allen) who investigates Treadstone from within. Even before Marie's death, Bourne is portrayed as haunted by the past, restaging the drama of identity lost. The espionage/action hero is necessarily detached from the social bonds of family and community.

The Female Spy in Espionage Action: Salt

Women in espionage movies are typically both improbable and mysterious creatures. Their talents as spies have long been linked to sexuality rather than action, encapsulated in the image of the spy as "Mata Hari."[2] The developing function of women within the Bond films has been the subject of much comment both scholarly and popular. Of their literary source Rosie White observes, "the purpose of women in Fleming's fiction is to certify the hero's masculinity" (2007: 30). Some Bond films have extended the figure of the so-called "Bond girl" into a more involved assistant role or even employed female action heroes, for example casting Michelle Yeoh (already well known for her action roles in Hong Kong films) as a Chinese spy in *Tomorrow Never Dies* (1997), or Halle Berry as an NSA agent in *Die Another Day* (2002).

---

[2]   Mata Hari was a Dutch exotic dancer executed for spying during World War I, reinforcing associations of sexuality and espionage. White (2007) discusses her life and transmutation into cinema.

Espionage provides a generic frame in which female action can be staged, one that foregrounds themes of disguise coupled to costume and glamour. Television has certainly played a part here. Just as Fox's *24* (2001–2010) demonstrated the popularity of the improbably tough male cop/government agent as action hero, the ABC series *Alias* (2001–2006) revived fantastical television espionage with a bewildering narrative of double crosses and action sequences (as well as science fiction elements) centered on the character of Sydney Bristow (Jennifer Garner). For White, the show represents a commentary on public femininity with its "juxtaposition of fast-paced action and soft focus melodrama." She argues that the action sequences in *Alias* operate, like the numerous costumes worn by Garner as Bristow, as a source of "scopophilic pleasure." It is telling that she regards the "fetishistic costumes and Hong Kong style action sequences" (2007: 127) as performing equivalent work, that of making a spectacle out of the female body. Certainly Bristow's on-going attempts to reconcile personal and professional identities – and the disguises and deceptions that this involves – speak to a concern that frequently accompanies female characters in action narratives: that they will somehow be rendered unwomanly or unfeminine if detached from emotional connections. That concern is registered in the seemingly inevitable requirement to *explain* female action. Such explanation underlines a culturally conservative film industry that both exploits and simultaneously contains the alluring yet potentially troubling image of female agency that the spy represents.

Like *Alien* some 30 years previously, *Salt* (2010) generated considerable comment because the lead role was initially written for a male character (Tom Cruise was attached to the project) before being taken by Angelina Jolie, a star with a well-established action profile from her role as the video game adventurer in *Lara Croft: Tomb Raider* and as Fox in the comic book adaptation, *Wanted* (2008). Jolie's desire to play a Bond figure rather than a supporting female role in a Bond film was reported in a number of press profiles and reviews; presumably her star power and action/fantasy credentials enabled that possibility with the film's international commercial success indicating the continuing appeal of such espionage scenarios. Certainly the Bond analogy was one identified by critics, with the *Hollywood Reporter* observing "Angelina Jolie, for all intents and purposes is James Bond in her new film *Salt*."

Promotion for *Salt* focused on questions of identity with posters featuring a close up of Jolie's face and the question, "Who is Salt?" As this suggests the film, like *The Bourne Identity*, foregrounds the deception and uncertainty that pervades the espionage narrative.

Salt commences two years before the primary action with an uncompromising scene of torture. This is familiar territory for the action film in which torture underlines the toughness of the action hero. Held in a North Korean prison, Salt's battered face and exposed body suggest her vulnerability while her repeated protestations that she is "not a spy" suggest fear rather than defiance. Salt's release is

(a)

(b)

PLATE 10.2a and b Evelyn Salt (Angelina Jolie) pictures the woman in espionage as intelligent, mysterious, even possibly duplicitous and as an extraordinary action hero (below): *Salt* (2010, directed by Phillip Noyce and produced by Columbia Pictures, Relativity Media, Di Bonaventura Pictures and Wintergreen Productions).

secured by the besotted Mike (August Diehl), an expert on spiders with whom Salt had been getting involved as part of her cover. As they are driven away, Mike declares his love and Salt declares her status as a spy. Two years later it is the couple's wedding anniversary. While a colleague jokingly refers to her as "Mata Hari," Salt is defined within the film not as a seductress but in terms of a marital status that frames and qualifies her role as spy. Early on the villainous Orlov (Daniel Olbrychski) remarks on her wedding ring "a husband must be a distraction for a female intelligence officer." Salt is indeed distracted by husband Mike for whom she has opted to work in the office ("pushing papers") rather than in the field, telling colleague Ted Winter (Liev Schreiber) that on her last time out she "was homesick."

This opposition between the female spy as seductress and Salt's characterization as both tough (as in the torture scene that opens the film) and domestic chimes with the film's at times bewildering narrative of concealed identity, treachery and double agents. The plot turns on the existence of a Soviet-era program by which numerous children have been raised as loyal to Orlov and positioned through the American establishment, ready for the arrival Day-X at which point they will act to trigger war between the two nations. It is revealed that Evelyn Salt was one of these children, although her loyalty is ultimately to the United States rather than Russia. The unreliability of those in charge – a familiar theme of action cinema – frames Salt's heroic solo endeavors. Her motivation remains obscure to other characters within the film and to audiences. For example, she seems to be responsible for the Russian President's death: only at the film's climax is it revealed that he is not dead but has been immobilized him with spider venom (knowledge gleaned from husband Mike). Such fantastical twists allow the film to play with its questions of identity and loyalty, questions that are persistently overlaid with the allied question of the gender conformity of the female spy. In the initial scenes Salt is driven to escape by her concern for Mike. Later, she will tell Orlov that she married Mike as a cover ("I did it to appear normal"). Once Mike is killed in front of her as a test of loyalty, Salt has nothing to lose. She proceeds to seize weapons and kill not only Orlov but all the sleeper agents who have greeted her as a comrade/sister.

The appearance of affection and intimacy in the service of professionalism is central to Hollywood cinema's construction of the spy.

Salt's plausible displays of emotion and connection – with Mike, Orlov and Ted (also a sleeper agent, unbeknownst to her) – are incompatible. Authenticity is expressed exclusively through action. In the action sequences Salt demonstrates her professionalism and capacity for violence whatever her affiliation. The film's first action sequence features Salt breaking out of the CIA building, tracked on surveillance cameras and pursued by greater numbers she uses initiative: shedding her heels Salt blocks the cameras using a fire extinguisher; moving to the interrogation room she uses her underwear to block the cameras before rigging up an improvised rocket launcher using office furniture and chemicals. Salt makes straight for her apartment where it is obvious that Mike has been kidnapped; grabbing weaponry, necessary (and the family dog) she makes a daring escape, scaling the walls of her apartment building. Her transformation from smart suit and heels – office wear – to the field, an action scenario involving pursuit on foot, in and across vehicles demonstrates that, above all, Salt is ready for action. In the climactic action sequence in the President's bunker Salt is both disguised and cross-dressed, her physical efforts by this point almost superhuman. And yet not quite, as Roger Ebert noted in his positive review of the film:

> She [Jolie] brings the conviction to her role that such a movie requires. She throws herself into it with animal energy. Somehow, improbably, she doesn't come off as a superhero (although her immunity suggests one), but as a brave and determined fighter.

The final image is of the vengeful Salt' escaping through the snow into the woods around the Potomac River. Aided by CIA Agent Peabody, she embodies the alienated spy as action hero: able to perform amazing physical feats, primed for action and definitively out in the cold.

CHAPTER 11

SUPERHERO ACTION CINEMA: X-MEN (2000) AND THE AVENGERS (2012)

The adaptation of heroic figures from popular literature, folk tales and comic books is not new. Yet it is undoubtedly the case that the most commercially successful action films and franchises of the twenty-first century have been fantasy, superhero and comic book adaptations including the *X-Men* series (2000, 2003, 2006, 2009, 2011, 2013, 2014), *Spider-Man* (2002, 2004, 2007), rebooted as *The Amazing Spider-Man* (2012, 2014), the Dark Knight trilogy of Batman films (2005, 2008, 2012), *Iron Man* (2008, 2010, 2013), *The Incredible Hulk* (2008), *Captain America* (2011, 2014), *Thor* (2011, 2013) and *The Avengers* (2012). These superhero films form a distinct trend within the broader context of fantasy film. They are clearly action films of a particular sort, emphasizing spectacular set design, visual effects and action sequences that stage the extraordinary exploits of superheroes. Superhero films effectively couple the comic book universe – with its backstories, evolving

The Hollywood Action and Adventure Film, First Edition. Yvonne Tasker.
© 2015 John Wiley & Sons, Inc. Published 2015 by John Wiley & Sons, Inc.

characterization and bold design – with conventions and styles that have evolved through the Hollywood action cinema over decades.

We've seen in previous chapters how the hero of action cinema – whether male or female – is an individual of extraordinary capabilities. The "everyman" heroes familiar from 1980s and 1990s action movies are stronger, smarter or simply tougher than their allies and opponents. The action hero's superiority is expressed via his/her enhanced body, intelligence or weaponry. An accelerating pattern of action sequences both demonstrates and extends the hero's abilities so that by the climax stunts and combat sequences are more demanding, louder and more spectacular underlining the enhanced hero at work. Although in superhero cinema the central characters are by definition extraordinary (even in some instances god-like), these action cinema patterns remain in place. Corresponding to the superheroes' enhanced powers the tasks faced are writ large, as for example, when Hulk faces Abomination or Iron Man tackles a monstrous version of his own metallic suit, a design adapted for warlike purpose by his business partner. As these examples suggest, themes of doubling are common in superhero cinema not only in the form of super-villains, but via more complex and long running associations between the hero and that which s/he opposes (Stark's wealth comes from the arms trade; Batman inhabits the shadows as much as his antagonists).

Moreover, the prominence of origin stories within superhero cinema suggests the continued importance of the theme of becoming-powerful that Purse regards as fundamental to action cinema. Superhero fictions are frequently concerned not only with origins but with the psychic and emotional struggles faced by the central characters in coming to terms with their abilities, powers and bodies. The physical changes they experience involve them in new and different relationships to loved ones and to the wider society. That is, the films reprise in spectacular form the thematic concerns of the outsider hero who fights on behalf of a community from which he (rarely she) is excluded. The temporary loss or distortion of a superhero's power – a repeated theme of superhero cinema – works in a comparable manner: the superhero turned bad becomes a threat or object of disgust rather than veneration (*Spiderman 3*) while the hero stripped of his powers (*Thor*) must adapt, albeit temporarily, to a body with limits.

The trope of the secret identity and of the equation of power with a costume or uniform that is put on for public performance is richly resonant. This device is distinct from the disguises of espionage action in which multiple identities are performed and set aside. Superhero fictions may involve concealment, identities that are hidden and those that are put on with the costume, but these are consistent. The interaction or conflict between these identities (Banner/Hulk, Wayne/Batman, Parker/Spider-Man) is familiar material that can be developed dramatically or to comic effect. We've seen how authenticity is frequently equated with action in the genre: in moments of physical exertion the hero is in his/her element, the warrior who embodies violence. That very violence is at times rendered ambivalent such that the hero is potentially unstable or uncontainable – the scenario dramatized around the enhanced capacities of veteran John Rambo in *First Blood* or, rather differently, Dr Bruce Banner (Edward Norton) in *The Incredible Hulk*. The theme of dual identities – putting on the suit – complements the trope of the restless or wandering hero who has no place that is familiar from the Hollywood Western. Like the heroes of the various action genres discussed in this book, superhero figures from Spider-Man to Wolverine are characterized by an ambivalent relationship to both authority and society. In both these examples the hero has been transformed by their interaction with technologies and the institutions that develop them; Spider-Man, more or less inadvertently, Wolverine, grotesquely.

With their superheroic abilities, moral legibility (Batman being a notable exception) and pre-sold characters, superhero action movies are clearly in line with the commercial logic of Hollywood production. In terms of the formal and thematic development of the genre superhero films provide fascinating sites of action. Their emphasis on rendering a cinematic impression of extraordinary powers or abilities such as flight, as well as the representation of the body transformed and transforming is central to the visual and thematic impact of these films. Evolving technologies of digital imaging are showcased in the superhero film, facilitating the cinematic representation of the comic book's dynamic framing.

The reinvigoration of superhero action depends on and has in turn facilitated significant advances in digital imagery. Yet Purse rightly cautions against too much emphasis on novelty in discussions of such technologies and the images they generate. She cites an essay on American cinema by German essayist Clare Goll; written in 1920, the assessment is strikingly familiar: "What is happening or rather racing by on the screen can be longer be called plot. It is a new dynamic, a breathless rhythm, action in an unliterary sense" (2011: 22). For Purse what is significant is that digital imaging technologies enable filmmakers to enhance the genre's core themes of the mastery of space and the embodiment of power. Her discussion of the proliferating use of speed ramping in the wake of *The Matrix* emphasizes the effects' relationship to these themes:

> ...the most common use of speed ramping is to enable an inten-
> sified focus on the body in motion, foregrounding the gestures
> of mastery the action body adopts during the flow of action by
> slowing them down radically until they almost register instead as
> static postures of mastery. (2011: 68)

These visual techniques use pace to evoke difference in the context of the familiar – an action shot slowed draws out aesthetic qualities and narrative significance. Such techniques suggest a distinctive rela-tionship to the comic book aesthetic that involves the graphic repre-sentation of movement and power, a series of frames that powerfully evoke action and emotion. Unsurprising then that superhero cinema has become such a prominent component of contemporary action.

Mutants and Others: X-Men

The wave of twenty-first century superhero action arguably com-menced with *X-Men* (2000).[1] A number of successful sequels and pre-quels followed including *The Wolverine* (2013) and *X-Men: Days of Future Past* (2014). The *X-Men* films revolve around tensions between mutants and humans, in turn generating conflict between mutants who adopt different responses to human hostility. In *X-Men* Senator Kelly (Bruce Davison) leads a campaign to establish mutant registration; we see him playing on popular fears that mutants with dangerous abilities may be hiding in plain sight, generating a climate of fear and danger.

---

[1]   Comic book adaptations had of course achieved a high profile in earlier decades – for example, Superman in the 1970s and early 1980s, Batman in the 1990s. These films varied from the clean-cut hero to the dark, surreal and com-plex. While superheroes such as Batman and Superman date their comic book origins to the 1930s, *X-Men* was first produced by Marvel comics in 1963.

Despite the subsequent existence of a ministry of mutant affairs and the official recognition this implies, *X-Men: The Last Stand* centers on the development of a cure for mutants, suggesting an administration still determined not only to regulate but actively to eradicate a portion of the population. "Since when did we become a disease?" asks an outraged Storm (Halle Berry) at the news that a laboratory has developed a serum to suppress mutant genes. By contrast Rogue (Anna Paquin), who is unable to touch without damaging others, seeks out this cure suggesting division amongst mutants themselves.

Some mutants exhibit their difference visibly, while others have powers that are not immediately apparent. The villainous Mystique is a shapeshifter; lithe, blue and reptilian she is able to take on the form of any human, irrespective of race, gender or age. Played by Rebecca Romijn and later, Jennifer Lawrence, Mystique appears as if naked; like Wolverine she is both human and nonhuman, but unlike him she is eroticized as well as othered – exemplifying O'Day's model of the action heroine as both simultaneously "the erotic object of visual spectacle and the action subject of narrative spectacle" (2004: 205). Mystique's athleticism, strength and close-combat fighting style exploits both animal and martial arts imagery, while the chief visual effect associated with her is a gradual transformation from one form to another. Mystique reveals herself as violent, seductive and powerful; cumulatively her character is defined by physical instability and deception.

In the film world mutants are grouped less by physicality or ability but according to their alignment with either Professor Charles Xavier (Patrick Stewart), or Magneto (Ian McKellen) and his Brotherhood of Mutants. Professor Xavier has established a school for young mutants, also effectively a refuge to which mutants can go to escape the castigation of the human world. Magneto, by contrast, rejects Xavier's approach of training and containing mutant power, arguing that mutants and not humans "are the future." To ensure that future, Magneto develops a weapon that artificially induces mutation – experimenting on Senator Kelly who dies grotesquely when his body rejects the mutation. Overcome by the X-Men, Magneto's parting shot is that he will fight the coming war "by any means necessary," an evocation of Malcolm X's famous speech on the challenges of combating racism in America.

This reference to American history is telling. While action has given greater prominence than other Hollywood genres to Black and Asian performers, the vast majority of heroic roles in comic franchises are white; some African-American characters occupy supporting roles, such as the character of James Rhodes/War Machine in the Iron Man series (Terrence Howard in the first film, Don Cheadle subsequently). The *X-Men* world, first published in comic book form in 1963, emerged from a cultural context of contestation on the meaning of race in America. Despite these associations with discourses of race and racism, the *X-Men* films – like the majority of comic book franchises – offer a distinctly white world. The multi-racial Storm, her role as much maternal as action-oriented, only partially conveys the elemental power of the comic book character. She remains largely relegated to the background of action sequences, associated with static poses rather than the movement that is typically associated with power in action cinema (rather differently to the comic book). Storm takes on the running of the school following Xavier's death in *Last Stand* underlining her position of authority amongst mutants. Yet action centers on Wolverine (Hugh Jackman), whose regenerative powers and adamantium skeleton render him a spectacle of human vulnerability (his wounds are visible), strength (the muscular body on display, the wounds that heal before our eyes) and animal qualities (his claws, hidden until needed for battle).

PLATE 11.1 Human and non-human: action centers on Wolverine (Hugh Jackman) in *X-Men* (2000, directed by Bryan Singer and produced by Twentieth Century Fox Film Corporation, Marvel Enterprises, Donners' Company, Bad Hat Harry Productions, Springwood Productions and Genetics Productions).

While in many ways *X-Men* re-launched the superhero film as the most high profile form of spectacular, action blockbuster, its darkness and themes of exclusion and social violence demonstrated an intriguing thematic range. The premise of *X-Men*, that of mutants whose powers set them apart and who are mistrusted and feared by humans, is familiar territory within science-fiction, a genre in which the dramatization of the encounter between human and non-human invokes the damaging consequences of social prejudice and racial intolerance. Indeed these forces are explicitly evoked in *X-Men* via the presentation of oppression and violence as part of Magneto's back story; the first film opens with a dramatic and emotional representation of Magneto's separation as a young boy from his parents in a rain-soaked concentration camp. Although his powers distort the metal gates and barbed wire that divide them, he is ultimately overcome by German soldiers. This representation of the Holocaust is far from idle – indeed Magneto himself will recall it in *Last Stand* when he remarks on the number tattooed on his arm. Magneto's anger is framed by his experience of the violent consequences of racism, experiences echoed in the prejudice faced by the young characters in the film, notably Rogue. When Mystique assaults Senator Kelly – transforming from an innocuous disguise as his white male assistant - she hisses: "people like you are the reason I was afraid to go to school as a child." Mystique's visceral hatred of humans is, like Magneto's, grounded in experience. Indeed the film conveys effectively the exclusion and prejudice experienced by mutants from Wolverine being thrown out of a bar by hostile locals to the crowds who cheer on Senator Kelly's anti-mutant speeches. Parallels between the hatred of mutants and the treatment of immigrants are underlined in the final confrontation that takes place on Ellis Island, Wolverine and Sabretooth doing battle on the Statue of Liberty itself.

Superhero Spectacle: The Avengers

Grossing over $1.5 billion dollars and topping the year's domestic box office by some margin *The Avengers* (2012) is the superhero action film writ large. With a production budget of $220 million, the film was produced by Marvel Studios and distributed by Disney. Following the team storylines established in the Marvel Universe, *The Avengers* brings together a group of male superheroes – Iron Man (Robert Downey Jnr), Captain America (Chris Evans), Thor (Chris Hemsworth) and the Hulk (Mark Ruffalo), each of which had featured in previous Marvel Studios films – to protect the Earth from an alien attack led by Thor's brother Loki (Tom Hiddleston), a charismatic villain also introduced in an earlier film. Nick Fury (Samuel L. Jackson), Director of S.H.I.E.L.D., brings these superheroes together with agents Natasha Romanoff/Black Widow (Scarlet Johansson) and Clint Barton/Hawkeye (Jeremy Renner).

The Avengers is an effects and spectacle led film, culminating in a lengthy combat action sequence in which the team – finally working as a unit – battles alien forces through the streets of New York. The gleeful and spectacular destruction of property that is so characterization of action cinema is in full evidence in this climactic battle scene. The invading army descends via vast reptilian vehicles that snake through the streets, smashing the glass of office blocks. Smoke, debris, vehicles hurled and fires breaking out provides the backdrop for action with the heroes facing a vast army of alien warriors. The city is rendered a war zone, superhero action juxtaposed with shots familiar from news footage and, rather differently, war movies. In tackling these creatures, Hulk leaps up, between and through buildings that crumble and smash under his weight, while on the ground Captain America

PLATE 11.2 Recurrent images of Stark's face emphasize the human-technology interface: Robert Downey Jnr in *Iron Man 2* (2010, directed by Jon Favreau and produced by Paramount Pictures, Marvel Entertainment, Marvel Studios and Fairview Entertainment).

takes charge, rescuing civilians cornered by invaders. *The Avengers* thus revels in the exhilaration of agile and powerful human movement against an expansive scene of spectacle.

The interplay of actors and effects is central to the superhero film. A recurrent image of Tony Stark's face within the Iron Man suit, framed and overlaid by projected data, contextualizes images of Iron Man speeding through the air, damaged by collisions or even gracefully landing. The suit suggests man subsumed by machine; emphasizing the face (and the voice) provides a counter to that anonymity. The interplay between Stark and the suit that makes him "Iron Man" – not a secret but rather a celebrity identity – exploits the theme of transition and doubling so common in the genre: Banner and Hulk, Parker and Spider-Man. It also exemplifies the emphasis on human qualities and foibles that are such an important feature of contemporary superhero action cinema. Steve Rogers/Captain America, a super soldier created in World War II via an experimental serum, is stoic, physically stable and authoritative. Thor's demi-god status is signaled by both diction and muscle, Chris Hemsworth serving as a straight-man to the more playful persona of Stark. Robert Downey Jnr's Stark is both obnoxious and charming, his narcissism, humor and stubbornness all in play through action sequences. The Iron Man character foregrounds Stark's pleasure in the power the suit gives him, as well as his vulnerability when it fails (Hulk will save him as he plummets to the ground in *The Avengers*).

The Avengers invokes but is not overly burdened by science-fiction themes of overreaching humans engulfed by the unforeseen consequences of scientific experimentation. The film's narrative premise is that S.H.I.E.L.D.'s attempt to harness the power of the mysterious Tesseract attracts the hostile attention of alien forces. The same object had appeared in *Captain America*, harnessed by villain Red Skull to equip his army, a strategy that S.H.I.E.L.D. is covertly replicating in *The Avengers*. While Steve Rogers observes wryly of the Tesseract "you should have left it in the ocean," tampering with technology – futuristic, alien or magical – is both dangerous and yet absolutely fundamental to superhero fictions. *The Avengers* is no exception, foregrounding the technical and scientific expertise of Stark and Banner. Both owe their superhero status to these abilities, albeit in very different circumstances. Banner is invited in ostensibly not for "the other guy" but for his expertise on gamma radiation. It is Agent Barton – soldier rather than scientist – who understands that since the Tesseract is a "doorway into space" it can be tampered with from either side. Although the Tesseract is removed from Earth by Thor, experimentation is never seriously questioned in the superhero film; indeed at the close of *The Avengers*, it is suggested that the Earth has effectively laid down a marker to potential alien invaders – its unruly character as expressed in the opposition of the Avengers serving as a form of protection from attack.

If science run amok is not a major preoccupation, violence, antagonism and revenge are; the fraternal battles of Thor and Loki, and the latter's desire for power and revenge, fuel the invasion. Conflicts between superheroes form a significant dimension of the film's spectacle: Thor and Iron Man battle each other, their conflict demolishing the surrounding forest while Loki looks on in amusement. Similarly Banner and Stark are both cynical about authority, questioning the motivations of S.H.I.E.L.D. and resisting attempts to bring them together. Stark describes his condition as a "terrible privilege," causing consternation by encouraging Banner to "strut" and to enjoy his own condition.

To a large degree the action of *The Avengers* turns on the disparate group's ability to overcome their disagreements and to come together as a team; from a "handful of freaks" to a protective force that can be called on. In *Iron Man* weapons manufacturer Tony Stark constructs the prototype suit as a vehicle for escape from his captors in Afghanistan. Stark is comically awkward in his subsequent attempts to develop and employ the suit – and indeed to remove it. In *The Avengers*, technology is no significant challenge and the main obstacle to be overcome is Stark's arrogance and inability to work with others. The verbal sparring between Stark and Captain America, the protracted fight between Thor and Hulk, or earlier, that between Thor and Iron Man, each work to generate spectacular scenes that emphasize dysfunctional relations (as does Thor's on-going battle with Loki). Barton, whose mind has been possessed by Loki, is brought back to himself when, in a drawn out brawl that matches the two members of the team who lack superpowers, Romanoff delivers a blow to the head. In turn all this antagonism between the central characters defers the very action image promised by the promotional materials, one in which the superheroes and their allies work together.

On board S.H.I.E.L.D.'s flying base Thor's battle with Hulk is as destructive as the attack led by a possessed Barton. It is also intercut with the developing cooperation between Iron Man and Captain America. Under the pressure of attack, they work together to rebuild the engines. As we've seen, action cinema typically revolves around the necessary enhanced skills of an individual hero who finds him or herself to be the right person in the right place. *The Avengers* reworks the formula to the extent that all the heroes have different skills and conflicting temperaments. Each is required to avert the alien forces that threaten the Earth, but can only be effective if working together. The formula is a familiar one played out repeatedly in the WWII combat film: while the courage of individuals is vital, results are achieved when a team operates as one. No coincidence then that the final New York battle scenes evoke the war film with super soldier Captain America taking control.

In popular reviewing practice, an overreliance or heavy-handed use of CGI forms a common criticism of action/blockbuster films. Indeed it is in part in this context that in interviews and other ancillary material such an emphasis is placed on the extensive training under-taken by performers, the effort and expertise required to undertake the roles. While such techniques are of course essential to superhero action, *The Avengers* underlines the importance to the genre of inte-grating these spectacular elements with theme and performance. Concluding his study of action cinema, Lichtenfeld writes: "The films that *do* make real their heroes' emotional and physical experiences are charged with a sense of spontaneity. These films make conventions seem organic; they enact the genre's rituals without making them feel obligatory" (2007: 344). Throughout this book, I have insisted on the narrative and thematic significance of action sequences within the larger action cinema. Nowhere is this more evident than the twenty-first century superhero action film. Here, the interaction of performers with each other and with the digitally created sets and monsters with which they are confronted prove vital in retaining the action's defining dynamic of vulnerability and power.

High profile Hollywood movies such as *The Avengers* have tended to focus on male characters. There are, we should note, no shortage of female heroes in both the Marvel Universe and the Avengers team including Ms Marvel/Captain Marvel. The iconic history of DC

Comics' Wonder Woman, explored in Kristy Guevera-Flanagan's documentary *Wonder Women! The Untold Story of American Superheroines* (2012) suggests the continuing cultural uncertainty around female action; despite her longevity as a comic book hero and her undoubted cultural visibility, this superhero has yet to have a film showcase. Female heroes do appear in ensemble narratives – Storm in *X-Men*, Sue Storm/Invisible Woman in *Fantastic Four* – and more memorably in villainous roles, as with Mystique in *X-Men*. Perhaps the most high profile cinematic adaptations of female action are not from comic books at all but from the world of gaming – the figures of Lara Croft, and Alice in the *Resident Evil* series being those most extensively discussed. It would be rash to suggest that the world of gaming is more welcoming to women or to female characters than the cinema and yet superhero cinema tends to confirm the sorts of gender hierarchies that have been consistent features of the genre. Strong women are present yet oddly peripheral to superhero cinema. An example of sorts is provided by the shifting presentation of Pepper Potts (Gwyneth Paltrow) in the *Iron Man* films. She is repeatedly cast as a woman in peril (being rescued in all three films), while serving a key narrative role as assistant (retrieving information on Stark's behalf, for example), before being recast as quasi-action figure in *Iron Man 3*. Indeed her power to protect Stark in the film's climax stems – perversely – from her very status as woman in peril: the film's villain has subjected Potts

PLATE 11.3 Romanoff (Scarlet Johansson) in *Iron Man 2*: super-assassin rather than super-hero, her enhanced fighting skills draw on familiar action tropes.

to the same process he has used to enhance his own body, bestowing on her strength and regenerative abilities.

Of course *The Avengers* does feature a prominent female character in the form of Natasha Romanoff/Black Widow, a superspy with no superpowers albeit possessing precisely the sorts of enhanced capacity for action showcased in Jolie's role in *Salt*: that is, improbably tough without being actually superhuman, Romanoff is able to deceive and manipulate others in pursuit of knowledge. Introduced in *Iron Man 2* as S.H.I.E.L.D.'s undercover operative within the Stark Corporation, Romanoff is smart, sexual and skilled in combat. In *The Avengers*, Romanoff enacts feminine vulnerability to secure intelligence, employing her skills first against a clownish set of goons, then to bring in Bruce Banner and later to secure information from another deceptive and articulate figure, Loki. Black Widow is introduced in a position of seeming danger; bound to a precariously poised chair she is being interrogated, a scene of violence interrupted by a phone call from S.H.I.E.L.D.'s Phil Coulson (Clark Gregg). Romanoff's cool assertion that she is "working" – verbally inverting the power relations of the scene – is followed by a sequence in which she easily overcomes her captors, using her body and the chair to which she is bound to physically assert her superiority.

This sequence enacts the action trope of becoming-powerful once more, an initial impression of vulnerability supplanted by violence and decisive physical authority. In line with the intensifying character of challenge and performance that characterize the genre, by the final battle scenes in New York, Black Widow demonstrates an extraordinary athleticism; leaping and back-flipping on and off alien vehicles. While all this is prefigured in the sequence that introduces her character, Black Widow's incorporation into the Avengers team seems to renders her more than human. This is the visual and thematic terrain of contemporary action cinema: action bodies that perform extraordinary feats when necessary, movement through space, violence as source of both narrative and aesthetic pleasure, and the celebration of mastery that is in the process of being forged.

BIBLIOGRAPHY

Abel, R. (2004) "The 'culture war' of sensational melodrama, 1910–14," in Tasker, Y., ed., *Action and Adventure Cinema*, London: Routledge, pp. 31–51.

Addison, H. (2002) "Capitalizing their charms: Cinema stars and physical culture in the 1920s" *Velvet Light Trap* 50: pp. 15–35.

Allison, D. (2004) "*Donald Siegel,*" *Senses of Cinema*, http://sensesofcinema.com/2004/great-directors/siegel/ (accessed November 28, 2014).

Altman, R. (2000) *Film/Genre*, London: BFI.

Arnold, E. T. and Miller, E. L. (1986) *The Films and Career of Robert Aldrich*, University of Tennessee Press.

Aronstein, S. (1995) "Not exactly a knight: Arthurian narrative and recuperative politics in the 'Indiana Jones' trilogy," *Cinema Journal* 34(3): pp. 3–30.

Arroyo, J., ed. (2000) *Action / Spectacle Cinema*, London: BFI.

Ascheid, A. (2006) "Safe rebellions: Romantic emancipation in the 'Woman's Heritage Film'," *Scope: An Online Journal of Film Studies* 4.

The Hollywood Action and Adventure Film, First Edition. Yvonne Tasker.
© 2015 John Wiley & Sons, Inc. Published 2015 by John Wiley & Sons, Inc.

Atakav, E. and Tasker, Y. (2010) "The Hurt Locker: Male intimacy, violence and the Iraq war movie," (with Eylem Atakav), *Sine*, 1(2): pp. 57–70.

Balio, T. (1993) *Grand Design: Hollywood as a Modern Business Enterprise, 1930–1939*, Berkeley: University of California Press.

Basinger, J. (2002) *The World War II Combat Film: Anatomy of a Genre*, 2nd edition, Wesleyan University Press.

Bazin, A. (1995) *What is Cinema? Vol II*, University of California Press.

Bean, J. (2004) "Trauma thrills: Notes on early action cinema," in Tasker, Y., ed., *Action and Adventure Cinema*, London: Routledge, pp. 17–30.

Beltrán, M. (2004) "Más Macha: The new Latina action hero," in Tasker, Y., ed., *Action and Adventure Cinema*, London: Routledge, pp. 186–200.

Bigelow, K. (1991) Interview, *Monthly Film Bulletin* 58: p. 313.

Bignell, J. (2008) *An Introduction to Television Studies*, London: Routledge.

Boggs, C. and Pollard, T. (2008) "The imperial warrior in Hollywood: Rambo and beyond," *New Political Science* 30(4): pp. 565–578.

Bordwell, D. (2002) "Intensified continuity: Visual style in contemporary American film," *Film Quarterly* 55(3): pp. 16–28.

Brown, J. A. (1993) "Bullets, buddies, and bad guys: The 'action-cop' genre," *Journal of Popular Film and Television* 21(2): pp. 79–87.

Buscombe, E. (1988) *The BFI Guide to the Western*, London: Andre Deutsch/BFI Publishing.

Cameron, I. (1973) *Adventure in the Cinema*, Studio Vista.

Carroll, N. (1982) "The future of allusion: Hollywood in the seventies (and beyond)," *October* 20: pp. 51–81.

Chan, K. (2004) "The global return of the *Wu Xia Pian* (Chinese sword-fighting movie): Ang Lee's *Crouching Tiger, Hidden Dragon*," *Cinema Journal* 43(4): pp. 3–17.

Coulthard, L. (2007) "'Killing Bill' rethinking feminism and film violence" in Tasker, Y. and Negra, D., eds, *Interrogating Postfeminism: Gender and the Politics of Popular Culture*, Duke University Press, pp. 153–175.

Denby, D. (2003) "High seas," *The New Yorker*, July 28th www.newyorker.com/archive/2003/07/28/030728crci_cinema (accessed November 24, 2014).

Diawara, M. (1993) "*Noir* by noirs: Toward a new realism in black cinema," in Copjec, J., ed., *Shades of Noir*, London: Verso, pp. 261–278.

Dika, V. (2003) *Recycled Culture in Contemporary Art and Film: The Uses of Nostalgia*, Cambridge University Press.

Doherty, T. (1999) *Projections of War: Hollywood, American Culture and World War II*, 2nd edition, Columbia University Press.

Dunn, S. (2008) *"Baad Bitches" and Sassy Supermamas: Black Power Action Films*, University of Illinois Press.

Dyer, R. (2000) "Action!" in Arroyo, J., ed., *Action/Spectacle Cinema*, London: BFI, pp. 17–21.

Ebert, R. (1972) *"Dirty Harry,"* http://www.rogerebert.com/reviews/dirty-harry-1971 (accessed November 24, 2014).

Eberwein, R. (2010) *The Hollywood War Film*, Wiley-Blackwell.

Eisele, J. C. (2002) "The Wild East: Deconstructing the language of genre in the Hollywood easterns," *Cinema Journal* 41(4): pp. 68–94.

Eleftheriotis, D. (2004) "Spaghetti western, genre criticism and national cinema: Re-defining the frame of reference," in Tasker, Y., ed., *Action and Adventure Cinema*, London: Routledge, pp. 309–327.

Erb, C. (1998) *Tracking King Kong: A Hollywood Icon in World Culture*, Wayne State University Press.

Flanagan, M. (2004) "Get ready for *Rush Hour.* The chronotope in action," in Tasker, Y., ed., *Action and Adventure Cinema*, London: Routledge, pp. 103–118.

Fradley, M. (2012) "Why doesn't your compass work? *Pirates of the Caribbean*, fantasy blockbusters, and contemporary queer theory," in Ross, K., ed., *The Handbook of Gender, Sex and Media*, London: Wiley-Blackwell, pp. 294–312.

Guerrero, E. (1993) *Framing Blackness: African-American Images in Film*. Temple University Press.

Gunning, T. (1986) "The cinema of attractions: Early film, its spectator and the avant-garde," (1986) in Elsaesser, T., ed., *Early Cinema: Space, Frame, Narrative*, London: BFI, pp. 56–62.

Gross, L. (2000) "Big and loud" in Arroyo, J., ed., *Action/Spectacle Cinema*, London: BFI, pp. 3–8.

Hark, I. R. (1976) "The visual politics of *The Adventures of Robin Hood*," *Journal of Popular Film* 5(1): pp. 3–17.

Higham, C. and Greenberg, J. (1968) *Hollywood in the Forties*, London: Tantivy Press.

Hoberman, J. (1985) "Seasons in Hell," *Village Voice* 28th May: p. 66.

Jeffords, S. (1993) *Hard Bodies: Hollywood Masculinity in the Reagan Era.* New Jersey: Rutgers University Press.

Kael, P. (1972) "Dirty Harry," *New Yorker*, 15th January.

Kaminsky, S. (1974) *American Film Genres*, Nelson-Hall.

Karnes, D. (1986) "The glamorous crowd: Hollywood movie premiers between the wars" *American Quarterly* 38(4): pp. 553–572.

Kemp, P. (2000) "Stealth and duty," *Sight and Sound* December, http://old. bfi.org.uk/sightandsound/feature/96 (accessed November 28, 2014).

King, G. (2000) *Spectacular Narratives: Hollywood in the Age of the Blockbusters*, London: I.B. Tauris.

King, G. (2009) *Indiewood, USA: Where Hollywood meets Independent Cinema*, London: I.B. Tauris.

Kitzes, J. (1969/2007) *Horizons West: The Western from John Ford to Clint Eastwood*, London: BFI.

Klein, C. (2004) "Martial arts and the globalization of US and Asian Film industries," *Comparative American Studies* 2(3): pp. 360–384.

Knight, S. (2006) "Remembering *Robin Hood*," *European Journal of English Studies*, 10(2): pp. 149–161.

Krämer, P. (1998) "Women first: *Titanic* (1997), action-adventure films and Hollywood's female audience," *Historical Journal of Film, Radio and Television* 18(4): pp. 599–618.

Krämer, P. (2004) "It's aimed at kids – the kid in everybody": George Lucas, *Star Wars* and Children's Entertainment" in Tasker, Y., ed., *Action and Adventure Cinema*, London: Routledge, pp. 358–370

Krutnik, F. (1991) *In a Lonely Street: Film Noir, Genre, Masculinity*, London: Routledge.

Lichtenfeld, E. (2007) *Action Speaks Louder: Violence, Spectacle, and the American Action Movie*, 2nd edition, Westport, Connecticut: Praeger.

Lovell, A. (1975) *Donald Siegel: American Cinema*, London: BFI.

Mast, G. (1979) *The Comic Mind: Comedy and the Movies*, University of Chicago Press.

Mazzocco, R. (1982) "The supply-side star," *The New York Review of Books*, April 1st www.nybooks.com/articles/archives/1982/apr/01/the-supply-side-star/ (accessed November 24, 2014).

McArthur, C. (1972) *Underworld U.S.A.* London: Secker and Warburg/BFI.

Mulvey, L. (1975) "Visual pleasure and narrative cinema," *Screen* 16.3 (Autumn): pp. 6–18.

Neale, S. (1999) *Genre and Hollywood*, London: Routledge.

Nollen, S. A. (1999) *Robin Hood: A Cinematic History of the English Outlaw and His Scottish Counterparts*, Jefferson: McFarland.

O'Day, M. (2004) "Beauty in motion: Gender, spectacle and action babe cinema," in Tasker, ed., *Action and Adventure Cinema*, London: Routledge, pp. 201–218.

Purse, L. (2011) *Contemporary Action Cinema*, Edinburgh University Press.

Richards, J. (1977) "The Swashbuckling Revival" *Focus on Film* 27: pp. 7–21.

Romao, T. (2004) "Guns and gas: Investigating the 1970s car chase film," in Tasker, Y., ed., *Action and Adventure Cinema*, London: Routledge, pp. 130–52

Sardar, Z. and Davies, M. W. (2010) "Freeze Framing Muslims," *Interventions* 12(2): pp. 239–250.

Sarris, A. (1985) "Review of Rambo," *Village Voice* 30th July, p. 53.

Schatz, T. (1981) *Hollywood Genres*, McGraw Hill.

Schrader, P. (1972) "Notes on film noir," *Film Comment* 8(1): pp. 8–13.

Singer, B. (2001) *Melodrama and Modernity: Early Sensational Cinema and Its Contexts*. New York: Columbia University Press.

Slotkin, R. (2001) "Unit pride: Ethnic platoons and the myths of American nationality," *American Literary History* 13(3): pp. 469–498

Stasia, C.L. (2007) "'My guns are in the Fendi!' The postfeminist female action hero," in Gillis, S, Howie, G. and Munford, R., eds, *Third Wave feminism: A Critical Exploration* 2nd edition, London: Palgrave McMillan, pp. 237–249.

Studlar, G. (1996) *This Mad Masquerade: Stardom and Masculinity in the Jazz Age*, New York, Columbia University Press.

Studlar, G. and Desser, D. (1990) "Never having to say you're sorry: *Rambo's* Rewriting of the Vietnam War," in Dittmar, L. and Michaud, G., eds, *From Hanoi to Hollywood: The Vietnam War in American Film*, Rutgers University Press, pp. 101–128.

Suid, L. (1978) "*The Sands of Iwo Jima*, the United States Marine, and the screen image of John Wayne," *Film & History* 8(2): pp. 25–41.

Tasker, Y. (1993) *Spectacular Bodies: Gender, Genre and the Action Cinema*, London: Routledge.

Taves, B. (1993) *The Romance of Adventure: The Genre of Historical Adventure Movies*. Jackson: University Press of Mississippi.

Teo, S. (2005) "Wuxia redux: *Crouching Tiger, Hidden Dragon* as a model of late transnational production," in Morris, M., Leung Li, S. and Chan Ching-kiu, S., eds, *Hong Kong Connections: Transnational Imagination in Action Cinema*, Duke University Press/Hong Kong University Press, pp. 191–204.

Thomas, T. (1976) *The Great Adventure Films*, New Jersey: Citadel Press.

Thompson, R. (2000) "Dirty Harry," *Senses of Cinema*, http://sensesof cinema.com/2000/cteq/dirty/ (accessed November 24, 2014).

Tibbetts, J. C. (1996) "The choreography of hope: The films of Douglas Fairbanks Snr," *Film Comment* 32(3): pp. 51–55.

Vojković, S. (2009) "Reformulating the symbolic universe: *Kill Bill* and Tarantino's transcultural imaginary," in Warren Buckland, ed., *Film Theory and Contemporary Hollywood Movies*, New York: Routledge, pp. 175–191.

Wallace, R. (1938) "He robbed the rich and gave to the poor," *Silver Screen* 8(2): pp. 28–29.

Warshow, R. (1964) *The Immediate Experience: Movies, Comics, Theatre and Other Aspects of Popular Culture*, Anchor Books.

White, R. (2007) *Violent Femmes: Women as Spies in Popular Culture*, London: Routledge.

Williams, T. (2004) "*The Dirty Dozen:* The contradictory nature of screen violence" in Tasker, Y., ed., *Action and Adventure Cinema*, pp. 345–357.

Winston Dixon, W. (1998) *The Transparency of Spectacle*, SUNY.

Zoglin, R. (1985) "An outbreak of Rambomania," *Time* June 24th: pp. 52–53.

INDEX

The Hollywood Action and Adventure Film, First Edition. Yvonne Tasker.
© 2015 John Wiley & Sons, Inc. Published 2015 by John Wiley & Sons, Inc.

White, Rosie, 174, 175

White Heat, 128

Wild Bunch, The, 38, 160

Williams, Tony, 38–9, 101

Willis, Bruce, 11, 113, 138, 145

Wolverine, The, 182

women 24–7, 32–3, 42–3, 52,
54–5, 62, 64–8, 86–7, 128–9,
132–4, 153, 155–7, 158–63,
172–8, 189–91

Wonder Woman (television), 26

Wonder Women! The Untold Story
of American Superheroines, 190

Wong, Anna May, 79–80

X2, 6

X-Men, 64, 68, 179, 182–5, 190

X-Men: Days of Future Past, 182

X-Men: The Last Stand, 63, 183,
184, 185

Yeoh, Michelle, 174